THE LEARNING PYRAMID:
POTENTIAL THROUGH PERCEPTION

NITA R. NUNN
Heritage Hall Private School

CHARLES R. JONES
Texas Tech University

THE LEARNING PYRAMID: POTENTIAL THROUGH PERCEPTION

CHARLES E. MERRILL PUBLISHING COMPANY

A Bell & Howell Company   *Columbus, Ohio*

EDUCATION
LIBRARY

THE SLOW LEARNER SERIES
edited by Newell C. Kephart, Ph.D.

Published by
Charles E. Merrill Publishing Co.
A Bell & Howell Company
Columbus, Ohio 43216

International Standard Book Number: 0-675-09083-0

Library of Congress Catalog Card Number: 72-78031

1 2 3 4 5 6 7 8 9 10—79 78 77 76 75 74 73 72

Printed in the United States of America

Preface

The Learning Pyramid: Potential Through Perception has been developed as a learning program for children with specific learning disabilities and is the result of more than three years of intensive observation of children with learning disabilities, detection of their specific deficits, and the development of activities and routines designed to eliminate or compensate for each deficit. Essential for children with learning disabilities, the program also has proved to be of value to every child, regardless of the area of exceptionality wherein he may fall, in establishing the basic motor skills necessary in forming a sound foundation for the total learning process.

A portion of the program initially was implemented in a public school setting in Lubbock, Texas, during the 1967–1968 school year. The program in its entirety first was presented at Heritage Hall Private School for Children with Learning Disabilities in Lubbock. At the present time, the program has been implemented into more than 750 individual school programs throughout the United States and in a pilot program in England.

The text, *The Learning Pyramid: Potential Through Perception,* has been used as an instructional guide by the classroom teacher in both public and private school settings with regular classes and remedial classes as well as in clinical settings for individual and group therapy. It has proved to be valuable resource material in the development of adaptive physical education programs and is presently being used as a text on the college level in teacher preparation programs.

Chapter 1 identifies and establishes those children with whom we are concerned, suggests the characteristics and manifestations of the child, and defines learning as related to the LEARNING PYRAMID upon which the entire program has been developed. In this chapter the rationale and objective of the program is established, thus giving a basic concept upon which instruction is founded.

Chapters 2 through 5 offer a step-by-step guide which may be used in implementation and administration of the program. Here the program has been divided into four areas of instruction:

> Perceptual Motor Activities
> Auditory Motor Activities
> Ocular Motor Activities
> Body and Space Awareness Activities

In addition, each of the activities listed under the above areas has been outlined according to the following:

> Equipment
> Objective
> Student Instruction
> Teacher Instruction

Under Student Instruction and Teacher Instruction the directions are very specific and on a very elementary level. The purpose here is twofold. First, difficulty in following directions and difficulty in repeating an activity when directions are given in a different manner each day is a primary deficit found in children with learning disabilities. Second, giving directions in a simplified manner and giving them in exactly the same manner and tone each day is a part of the structure of the program which must be established.

Chapter 6 is concerned with implementation of the program in both a public school setting and a private school setting. Areas discussed are related to the following:

> Personnel
> Plant
> Length of Period
> Length of Program
> Equipment

The chapter includes specific and simplified specifications for the building and construction of all equipment and materials needed in carrying out the program. "Teaching Guidelines," is a listing of twenty very specific rules to be followed in assuring the structure and success of the program.

A glossary of terminology used throughout the program is included. Although professional terminology has been kept to a minimum, the need for clarification and identification of terms used still exists. Confusion in the administration of a program of this type often has been the result of inappropriate use of terminology between administrator and teacher and, even more important, between teacher and parent.

Grateful acknowledgement is made to those persons whose contributions helped make this presentation possible. Appreciation is extended to Dr. James Winter for his direction in the area of Visual Motor Development, and to Dr. Mary Owens for her active participation in the present program at Heritage Hall. Dr. Max Manley made possible the initial implementation of the program in a public school setting, and Miss Tina Bateman contributed endless effort in the pre- and post-testing of the public school research program. A special note of thanks is expressed to Miss Kathryn Peddy, not only for her efforts directed toward research on each of the individual perceptual activities, but also in the final preparation of this manuscript.

Many others, through their constructive criticism and evaluation of the program, have helped make this a comprehensive and workable guide for teaching and for laying the foundation for learning. Hopefully, through continued research, detection of the more specific deficit areas in the individual child, and through the development of new methodology, our children will be afforded an educational program to meet their total needs. At that time in the future, the child will be able to accept himself, realize the worth of his being, and become a contributing member of the society into which he was born.

NITA R. NUNN
CHARLES R. JONES

Lubbock, Texas
May, 1972

Contents

chapter 1   The Learning Pyramid   3

chapter 2   Perceptual Motor Activities   9

chapter 3   Auditory Motor Activities   35

chapter 4   Ocular Motor Activities   53

chapter 5   Body and Space Awareness Activities   79

chapter 6   Implementation of Program   103

              General References   121

              Glossary   125

THE LEARNING PYRAMID: POTENTIAL THROUGH PERCEPTION

chapter 1

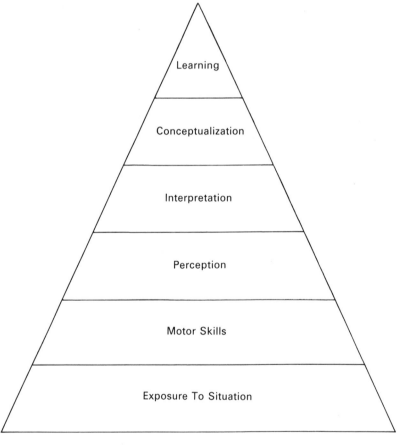

The Learning Pyramid

The Learning Pyramid

INTRODUCTION

As an infant is brought into the world, the first responses we detect are motor in nature . . . a clenched fist exploring space . . . eyes adjusting to light . . . a spontaneous, healthy cry . . . each a behavioral response to a given stimulus. These motor responses, during the first moments of life, are the basis of the learning process elevating the child from one level of achievement to the next until his full potential has been realized.

All too often it is assumed that from the initial motor responses a sequential learning process will follow. Such is not always the case as evidenced by the child we now identify as one with a specific learning disability. If, during the prenatal development of the fetus, there is an interruption in the development of the neurological system, varying degrees of dysfunction will be noted. The severity of the interruption will determine the degree of dysfunction which, in turn, identifies the learning disability in the individual child.

A child with one or more learning disabilities may be observed to manifest a number of behavioral characteristics. The degree to which each characteristic is observable will vary within each individual child and seldom will all characteristics be observed in any one child. The characteristics suggested in this chapter should serve only as a guide. It should be noted that each of the characteristics may be indicative of a learning disability, but after close evaluation, be more applicable to an entirely different area of exceptionality.

With research providing us with the knowledge that children with learning disabilities almost without exception will manifest a deficit in the area of perceptual motor development, we can conclude that a program in perceptual development is an integral and necessary part of the educational program if complete learning is to evolve.

The overall objective of the program is to develop in each child the basic perceptual motor skills necessary for progressive, upward achievement in the classroom and to make the transference of these skills into each academic learning situation, keeping in mind that each individual skill is merely a component part in the total growth and learning process of the child. Consideration should be given, therefore, to the program's application and value to children in all areas of exceptionality as well as to the child in the regular classroom situation.

The Learning Pyramid: Potential through Perception is not the answer to every learning problem, nor will it assure the nonreader of successfully being able to read at the end of a year's training. Rather, it is simply another means by which readiness skills for learning in each of the academic areas may be developed and reinforced.

It is hoped that all who use this program—college instructor, classroom teacher, diagnostician, psychologist—will consider it only as a beginning; that each child will be observed, carefully evaluated and identified according to his own specific deficits, and activities then developed or those presented here enlarged upon in an attempt to meet the individual needs of each child.

THE CHILD DEFINED

Definitions for children with specific learning disabilities have become many and often varied in meaning. In too many instances a definition has been the result of singling out only a few of the more obvious characteristics of the child and identification has been determined on this basis.

For the purpose of this program we shall define the child with a specific learning disability as one with normal intelligence, but for whom it is impossible to achieve to his full potential in the normal classroom situation employing normal classroom methodology . . . the child who manifests a significant difference in his estimated potential to learn and his actual achievement . . . the child who is characterized by learning deficits in specific areas . . . all of which impede, or prevent entirely, the normal and expected learning process.

CHARACTERISTICS

As noted earlier, seldom will all of the following characteristics be found in a single child and in many instances some will be detected in the very normal child. The teacher must, therefore, proceed cautiously before labeling and tentatively identifying a child as one with a learning disability.

To assure the value of this information to the layman as well as the experienced educator, very specific manifestations have been listed rather than the more general categories of characteristics. The following, therefore, are for consideration by the teacher in helping identify the child with a specific learning disability:

hyperactivity	poor visual discrimination
distractibility	poor auditory discrimination
short attention span	right to left progression
short memory span	bottom to top progression
impulsiveness	poor body concept
emotional lability*	lack of space awareness
speech defect	poor general coordination
poor self concept	poor eye-hand coordination
poor concept formation	poor eye-foot coordination
faulty reasoning	mixed dominance
language deficits	crossed dominance
poor sequencing	laterality confusion
motor disorders	directionality confusion
normal or above intelligence	lack of rhythm

LEARNING AND THE LEARNING PYRAMID

Learning, as defined by Webster, is the "acquisition of knowledge or skill received by instruction or study." For the child with a specific learning disability a more comprehensive definition is perhaps necessary. Based on the *Learning Pyramid,* and in relation to this program, learning shall be defined as *exposure to one or more stimuli in a given situation; being in possession of the necessary motor skills with which to perceive, interpret,*

---

*As a result of repeated academic failure, inability to adjust socially, and the resulting poor self-concept of the child with a learning disability, a certain degree of emotional insecurity and instability is to be expected. If, however, the emotional disturbance appears to be the prime factor in the inability of the child to adjust academically and socially, the child must then be identified primarily as emotionally disturbed and placed accordingly, and secondarily as a child with a learning disability and academically programmed according to the specific deficit.

and accurately conceptualize through the sensory modalities; arriving at a solution, or motor action, acceptable to our present culture.

Learning is a *pyramid* of sequential steps beginning with an exposure to a given situation. Many children are deprived of the opportunity to learn because exposure has actually never taken place. One major objective of this program shall therefore be to simulate those experiences which may have been omitted.

There are those who will contend that motor skills follow, rather than precede, perception, interpretation, and conceptualization. Such contention may be proven to lack validity when we understand that the very basic motor skills, even though quite primitive and perhaps defective, are present in an infant at birth.

At any given step in the upward progression of the pyramid the total learning process may be halted. This step, then, is the goal toward which we must work before taking the child forward to the next step; therefore, keep in mind that perception, interpretation, conceptualization and the final capacity for learning are contingent upon the first two basic steps: exposure to a given situation and adequate motor skills to continue the upward climb. In the following activities it should be noted that there will be an overlapping of the objectives of each activity, which is an asset in that the child will be working toward the development of more than a single skill in each activity. In the teacher's instructions, however, the teacher will be asked to stress a particular skill and merely reinforce or call attention to the other skills which will have been stressed in other activities.

chapter 2

1. Exercise Cycle
2. Directional Commands
3. Space Patterns
4. Rhythm Steps
5. Rocking Board
6. Balance Board
7. Stair Steps
8. Puppets on A String
9. Indian Club Maze
10. Tumbling
11. Cadence
12. Take A Stance

Perceptual Motor Activities

Throughout the lifetime of an individual numerous experiences occur. The perception of the experience, however, is far more important than the experience itself as it relates to meaningfulness and a factual foundation for learning. Perception is the axiom of an experience . . . and motor movement is the beginning of all experience an individual encounters throughout life. Just as the behavioral manifestations of a child vary according to the manner in which he perceives himself, so will a child's behavioral manifestations vary according to the manner in which he perceives an experience. Deficits in the area of motor skills involving gross motor action and reaction are often the first significant indicators of an existing learning disability. A child's initial quest for learning experiences evolves around motor exploration and motor questioning. Inappropriate perceptual motor matches or distorted matches as a result of imperception will lead to the continuing development of false concepts and the resulting learning disability.

The following activities are designed to aid in the development of basic perceptual motor skills as a foundation for the acquisition of the higher skills of learning.

1. EXERCISE CYCLE

Equipment: Area large enough for children to form a circle with at least six feet between each child.

Objective: General coordination, physical fitness, laterality, directionality, rhythm, balance, ability to stop and start, sequencing, spacing, pacing, body control, body position in space.

Student Instruction:

I want all of you to form a circle in the middle of the room by joining hands. Now, drop hands and begin stepping backward until there is this much room between each of you. (Indicate amount of room.)

We will do the exercise cycle by following one another around the room in a circle. Keep your eyes on the back of the person in front of you, listen to my instructions, and follow my instructions. Stand up straight, feet together, hands by your side. Always begin on your left foot. *Ready:*

Step, step, step together hold; touch your toes and up; touch your toes and up.

Repeat
Step, step, step together hold; airplane to the left; airplane to the right.

Repeat
Step, step, step together hold; knee-bend and up; knee-bend and up.

Repeat
Step, step, step together hold; roll from the waist; roll from the waist.

Repeat
Step, step, step together hold; stretch to the sky; stretch to the sky.

Repeat
Step, step, step together hold; bounce, bounce and up; bounce, bounce and up.
Repeat

Teacher Instruction:

All of the objectives should be stressed throughout this activity, with a special emphasis placed on the child performing on the verbal command.

If the exercises are new to the children, the teacher should stop the cycle and demonstrate each just before it is executed for the first time.

Explanations of exercises are as follows:

1. Step, step, step together hold—Beginning with the left foot, three steps forward, bring the right foot up to the left foot and hold.

2. Touch your toes and up—With feet together, beginning with body in an erect position, bend from the waist, touch the toes with the finger tips and return to erect body position.

3. Airplane to the left (or to the right)—With feet together, beginning with body in an erect position, raise both arms parallel to the floor. Without bending arms and without changing foot position, swing the arms as far to the left as possible and then as far to the right as possible.

4. Knee-bend and up—With feet together, beginning with body in an erect position, a deep knee-bend, keeping the back straight and bringing the arms up until they are parallel to the floor and in front of the body, returning then to erect body position.

5. Roll from the waist—With feet together, beginning with body in an erect position, and arms by the side, bend forward from the waist, roll the body to the left, around to the back, to the right, back to the front position, returning then to erect body position.

6. Stretch to the sky—With feet together, beginning with body in an erect position, stretch the arms high above the head, raising the body on tiptoe, returning then to erect body position.

7. Bounce, bounce and up—With feet together, beginning with body in an erect position, bend forward from the waist as far as possible without bending the knees and with arms dangling. Bounce twice from the waist toward the floor, returning then to erect body position.

Extreme structure and no talking. All commands given in rhythmic manner.

Directional Commands

2. DIRECTIONAL COMMANDS

Equipment: Area large enough for children to form two lines with each
child facing the instructor and with at least two feet between each child when arms are outstretched.

Objective: Laterality, directionality, following direction on command, rhythm, preciseness in movement, visual fixation
while body is in motion.

Student
Instruction: I want this half of the group (indicate which half) to form
a line which will reach from this side of the room to that
side of the room and with each of you facing me. Stretch
your arms out to the sides of your body and then move
apart from one another until there is this much room
between each of you (indicate amount of room.)

(The same instruction is then given to the remaining half
of the class, having them form their line in front of the first
group.)

I am going to call out different commands which will be directions. On each command I want you to show me the direction by moving either one or both arms.

Stand up straight, feet together, hands by your side. *Ready:*

To the left; to the right; up above; down below; in the back; in the front; all around. (Repeat, changing sequence of commands.)

Teacher Instruction: Emphasis should be placed on preciseness of movement and the rhythm with which each command is carried out.

It also should be stressed that a visual fixation must be held and that the eyes should not follow the direction in which the arms are moving.

Extreme structure and no talking. All commands given in rhythmic manner.

3. SPACE PATTERNS

Equipment: Area large enough for children to form two lines with each child facing the teacher and with at least two feet between each child.

Objective: Laterality, directionality, rhythm, pacing, change of pace, spacing, following direction on command, preciseness of movement, posture, body control, balance, sequencing, ability to stop and start.

Student Instruction: I want this half of the group (indicate which half) to form a line which will reach from this side of the room to that side of the room and with each of you facing me. Stretch your arms out to the sides of your body and then move apart from one another until there is this much room between each of you. (Indicate amount of room.)

(The same instruction is then given to the remaining half of the class, having them form their line in front of the first group.)

In this activity, we are going to be marching. We shall all need to be doing exactly the same thing at exactly the same time. We shall be marching in many different directions, all moving at the same time. We shall be making patterns on the floor with our feet. Think about the patterns you are making as you follow each command. Listen to the sounds you make with your feet.

Stand up straight, feet together, hands by your side. *Ready:*

L. together, L. together, L. together, hold.
R. together, R. together, R. together, hold.
L. together, Front together,
R. together, Back together,
L. together, L. together, L. together, hold.
Front, front, front together,
R. together and hold.
Front, front, front together,
R. together and hold.
All together to the rear face,
Front, front, front together hold.

(Quicken Pace)

L. together hold, R. together hold,
L. together, L. together, L. together hold.
R. together hold, R. together hold,
All together to the rear face; *at ease.*

Teacher
Instruction: This activity will be difficult in the beginning for most students and only a small portion of the routine should be attempted, and then mastered, before proceeding to the next part.

Stress spacing and change of pace, starting and then coming to a complete halt, rhythm, body steering, sequencing, and the entire group moving together as "one."

Explanation of terminology is as follows:

1. L. (Left) together hold—The left foot is moved to the left and planted firmly; right foot is then drawn to the left foot and held in position.

2. R. (Right) together hold—The right foot is moved to the right and planted firmly; left foot is then drawn to the right foot and held in position.

3. Front together—Left foot steps out and forward and is planted firmly; right foot is then drawn to the left foot and held in position.

4. Back together—Right foot is taken out and back and is planted firmly; lcft foot is then drawn to the right foot and held in position.

Extreme structure and no talking. All commands given in rhythmic manner.

4. RHYTHM STEPS

Equipment: Two-by-two inch crosses constructed of one-half inch colored tape and placed on the floor according to Chapter 6, Diagram 1.

Objective: Sequencing, pacing, spacing, rhythm, eye-foot coordination, left-right progression, change in pacing, change in spacing, balance, general body coordination.

Student Instruction: Form a line just behind the first colored cross. I shall begin instruction with the word "and" at which time you will step lightly on the first cross with your *left* foot; on the second cross with your *right* foot, and so on until you have reached the end of the crosses.

When the crosses are close together, you will take a *small, fast,* step; and when the crosses are far apart, you will take a *large, slow,* step.

Remember what we have said about rhythm in everything we do: in our walking, in our talking, in our reading, in our writing. Try to travel to the end just as smoothly as you can. I shall clap my hands in rhythm with you. *Ready:*

Teacher
Instruction: Emphasis should be placed on the fact that rhythm can be
                   maintained even though pacing and spacing are changed.
                   Encourage posture to be erect as there is a tendency for the
                   child to lean forward toward the floor especially when
                   there is a space awareness deficit. Auditory reinforcement
                   is given through the teacher's clapping and may also be
                   given with the teacher's calling "Left, Right, Left, Right,"
                   etc. Once the activity is more familiar, encourage the chil-
                   dren to clap with you.

                   Extreme structure and no talking. All commands given in
                   rhythmic manner.

5. ROCKING BOARD

Equipment: Rocking board constructed according to Chapter 6, Dia-
                   gram 2; 8½-inch playground ball.

Objective: Balance, body coordination, directional awareness, eye-
                   hand coordination, rhythm, sequencing.

Student
Instruction: Line up behind the rocking board, one behind the other.
                   You will each take your turn and while one is on the
                   rocking board, the remainder of the class should watch
                   carefully. Remember that you learn by watching as well as
                   by doing.

                   I want the first student to step up to the rocking board and
                   place his left foot just a little off-center on the rocking
                   board. Quickly, but carefully, lift your right foot onto the
                   rocking board just a little off-center on the other side of the
                   rocking board. Move your feet just the slightest bit until
                   you have your balance.

                   We are going to be thinking about, and working with, six
                   directions all at the same time. First begin rocking the
                   board in a left to right or side to side motion by slightly
                   bending one of your knees and then the other.

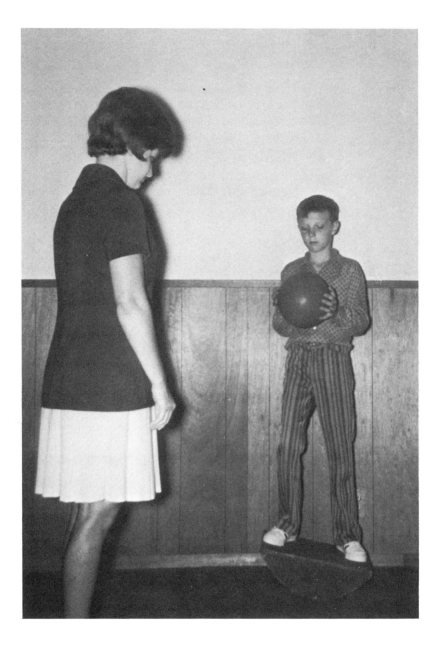

Rocking Board

While you are continuing this motion, I shall hand you a rubber ball. You will now begin bouncing the ball up and down to yourself.

Now that you are able to combine these two activities, I want you to stop bouncing up and down to yourself and begin bouncing the ball out to me and I shall bounce it back to you. Let's practice this now.

We are now ready to put together all of the activities into a pattern of rocking and bouncing, using all of your directions, keeping your balance, and keeping your rhythm. *Ready:*

Begin rocking from side to side, then
bounce to yourself; bounce to yourself;
out to me; in to you.
Bounce to yourself; bounce to yourself,
out to me; in to you.

*Teacher
Instruction:*   Balance is important in this activity. Emphasis should also be placed on rhythm and the sequence of the different directional activities.

Continue the routine on the rocking board with each child as long as balance is maintained and until you feel the student has established a rhythm.

As the child becomes more skilled, the teacher should vary the distance from the child; move forward, then backward, then forward again. The child will need to judge distance in how far out he must bounce the ball.

Extreme structure and no talking. All commands given in rhythmic manner.

6. BALANCE BOARD

Equipment: Balance board constructed according to Chapter 6, Diagram 3; 8½-inch playground ball; target.

Objective: Balance, body coordination, body awareness, body control in space, eye-hand coordination, directionality, laterality.

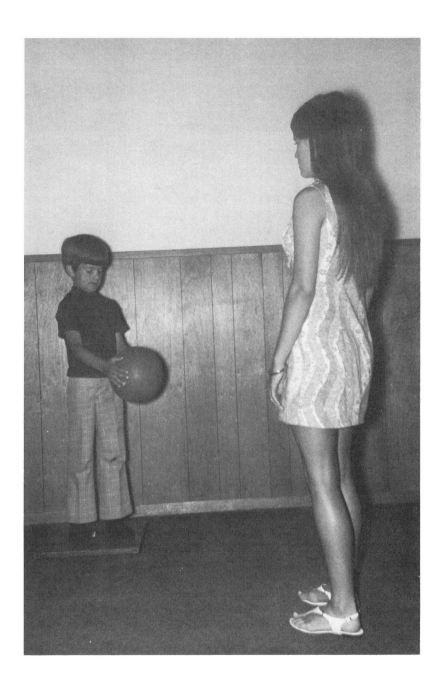

Balance Board

*Student
Instruction:* Line up behind the balance board, one behind the other. You will each take your turn performing a certain activity on the balance board. After each of you has had a turn, we shall go on to the next activity.

Part 1. I want the first student to step up to the balance board. Step on first with the left foot and then quickly, but carefully, with the right foot. Move your feet around on the board until you have your balance.

Now that you have your balance I am going to hand you the ball. Begin bouncing the ball on the floor in front of you, trying to bounce in rhythm. *Ready:* (Each child takes turn.)

Part 2. Step onto the balance board as you did before and try to get your balance. Once again I am going to hand you the ball. This time I want you to aim at the target on the wall in front of you and try to hit it with the ball. After you have thrown the ball, remain on the balance board so I may see that you still have your balance. *Ready:* (Each child takes turn.)

Part 3. Step onto the balance board as you did before and be sure that you have your balance. This time we are going to practice our directions as we did in our directional commands activity. *Ready:* (Each child takes turn.)

To the left, to the right;
Up above, down below;
In the front; in the back;
All around.

*Teacher
Instruction:* All objectives should be stressed with a special emphasis on not attempting the activities until balance has been attained.

The distance the target is placed from the balance board in Part 2 will vary with the age, size, and ability of the children.

In Part 3, repeat commands as long as child maintains balance and until directions have been properly indicated several times. Vary sequence of commands.

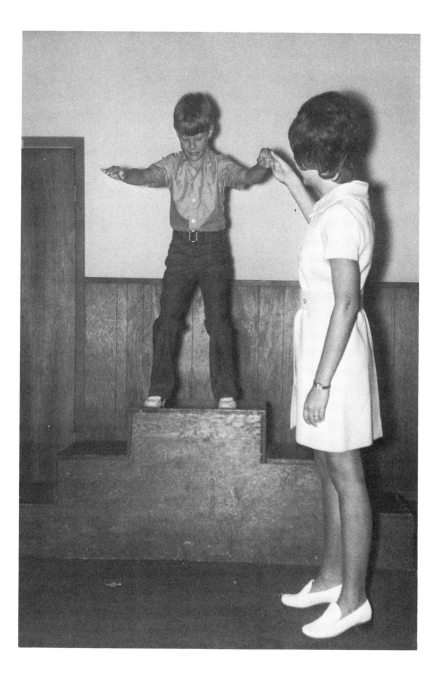

Stair Steps

21

As the children become more skilled in maintaining their balance, the base of the balance board may be changed to the smaller size, thus making balance more difficult.

Extreme structure and no talking. All commands given in rhythmic manner.

7. STAIR STEPS

Equipment: Stairs constructed according to Chapter 6, Diagram 4; five-by-five inch beanbag for each child.

Objective: Left-right progression, sequencing, balance, body coordination, laterality, body control, eye-foot coordination, directionality, body in space, pacing, spacing, alternation of body movements.

Student Instruction: Line up on this side of the stairs, one behind the other. You will each take your turn and only one student will be on the stairs at a time. While you are going up the stairs and while you are going down, I shall have my arm outstretched in front of you. I shall not let you fall. *Ready:*

Part 1. First we shall go up the stairs on this side and down on the other. Begin with your left foot, one foot on each step, taking two steps on the top level. Let's try to step in rhythm and this time your eyes may help you by watching your feet. *Ready:*

Left, right, left, right,
Down, down, and off.
(Each child takes turn.)

Part 2. We are now going to do exactly the same thing, only this time you may not watch your feet. Keep your eyes on the target in front of you on the wall. *Ready:*

Left, right, left, right,
Down, down, and off.
(Each child takes turn.)

Part 3. In our next activity you will go only to the top of the stairs. You will not go down the stairs. Instead, you will jump from the top of the stairs to the floor. This time you also will begin with your right foot rather than your left foot and for your two steps on the top level (indicate top level) you will turn your feet, placing them in position ready to jump toward the front or toward me. *Ready:*

Right, left, right, left, and jump.
(Each child takes turn.)

Part 4. Repeat Part 2 with beanbag on head of each child. Eyes straight ahead on target.

Part 5. Repeat Part 3 with beanbag on head of each child. Eyes straight ahead on target while ascending stairs and out into space when jumping.

Teacher
Instruction: All objectives should be stressed with an emphasis on spacing and pacing without visual reinforcement. Also emphasize lifting the body before jumping rather than just sliding off.

Extreme structure and no talking. Commands given in rhythmic manner.

8. PUPPETS ON A STRING

Equipment: Area large enough for children to lie on the floor with all limbs extended and with at least two feet between each child when in this position.

Objective: Laterality, directionality, general coordination, execution of movement on command, identification of body parts, rhythm, simultaneous movement of opposite body parts, abstraction.

Student
Instruction: I want this half of the class to form a line, with each of you facing me, at the back of the room, and with at least this

much space between each of you. (Indicate which half of class and amount of space to be left between each child.) I want the remainder of the class to form a line here, toward the front of the room, with each of you facing me, and with at least this much space between each of you. (Once again indicate where the line is to be and the amount of space to be left between each child.)

Now that you are in position, lie down on your backs, without moving the position of your feet; put your hands by your sides and your feet together.

You are going to be puppets and I am going to be the puppet master and pull the strings which will move your arms and legs. We are pretending, of course, that you are only puppets and you will make your arms and legs do just what I say, and nothing more.

I shall call out different commands. When I say "Left Arm," for example, you will simply lie still and think about that part of your body. Then when I say "Out," you will very swiftly move your left arm out and away from your body, sliding it along the floor, and back down beside your body on the word, "In." *Ready:*

Left arm, out and in.
Right arm, out and in.
Left leg, out and in.
Right leg, out and in.
Both arms, out and in.
Both legs, out and in.
Arms and legs, out and in.
Left arm, left leg, out and in.
Right arm, right leg, out and in.
Left arm, right leg, out and in.
Right arm, left leg, out and in.

Teacher
Instruction: All objectives should be stressed and it is important that the children are spaced correctly before the activity is begun.

All commands must be given in a rhythmic manner and with an emphasis on the words "Out" and "In." Emphasize also the "thinking" of the body part before "moving" the body part.

To eliminate the children learning the movements by rote, vary the order in which the commands are given.

Extreme structure and no talking.

9. INDIAN CLUB MAZE

Equipment: Six, eighteen-inch Indian clubs with room enough for the clubs to be placed in a line, one behind the other, with at least two feet between each club.

Objective: General coordination, spacing, pacing, eye-foot coordination, walking, running, jumping, hopping, skipping, rhythm, left-right progression.

Student
Instruction: I want all of you to line up, one behind the other, behind the line of Indian clubs. You will each travel through the maze of Indian clubs one at a time, and each time you will be traveling through in a different way. However, even though you will be traveling in a different way, you will always follow the same route, or same pattern. You will always start by going to the left of the first Indian club; to the right of the second Indian club; to the left of the third Indian club; and so on to the end of the line. *Ready:*

   Part 1.   Walking
   Part 2.   Running
   Part 3.   Jumping (both feet together)
   Part 4.   Hopping (left foot)
   Part 5.   Hopping (right foot)
   Part 6.   Skipping

Teacher
Instruction: Stress all objectives with an emphasis on left-right progression and a rhythmic manner in moving through the maze.

   Encourage the children to move as close to the Indian clubs as possible without knocking them over and to make movement through the maze a continuous progression.

For the very young children it may be necessary to first practice the six types of motion.

Extreme structure and no talking.

Tumbling

10. TUMBLING

Equipment: One tumbling mat at least six feet by fifteen feet.

Objective: Physical fitness, general coordination, body awareness, position in space, laterality, directionality, flexibility, eye-foot coordination, eye-hand coordination.

Student
Instruction: I want all of you to line up at this end of the tumbling mat, one behind the other.

                  We are going to do many different activities and stunts on the tumbling mat, but only one person may be on the mat at a time. I do not want the second student in line to begin his stunt until the first student is completely off the mat and returning to the end of the line.

I shall demonstrate each activity for you just before the first person in line begins his turn. *Ready:*

1. Log Roll
2. Somersault (forward)
3. Somersault (backward)
4. Cat Walk
5. Duck Walk
6. Crab Walk (forward)
7. Crab Walk (backward)
8. Inchworm
9. Cartwheel

Teacher
Instruction: Stress all objectives with an emphasis on proper body position for proper execution of activity and a continuous movement from one end of the mat to the other.

Under no circumstances should more than one child be on the mat at a time.

Extreme structure and no talking.

11. CADENCE

Equipment: Area large enough for children to form two lines with each child facing the instructor and with at least two feet between each child when arms are outstretched.

Objective: Laterality, directionality, following direction on command, rhythm, precision in movement, body control, perception with and without visual reinforcement.

Student
Instruction: I want this half of the group (indicate which half) to form a line which will reach from this side of the room to that side of the room and with each of you facing me. Stretch your arms out to the sides of your body and then move

apart from one another until there is this much room between each of you (indicate amount of room.)

(The same instruction is then given to the remaining half of the class, having them form their line in front of the first group.)

I am going to call out different commands which will be directions. On each command I shall want you to show me the direction by turning your body a quarter turn. A quarter turn is this far (demonstrate a quarter turn.)

There will be many turns. They may be either to the left or the right. Do not begin to turn until you have heard each command.

Part 1. Stand up straight, feet together, hands by your side, eyes straight ahead. *Ready:*

Left face, right face; right face; left face; right face; left face; halt.

(Variations of the above are then given. Have the children note the direction they are facing when you say "Halt." Then show them the direction they should be facing if all turns had been made correctly.

Part 2. (Repeat Part 1, giving same instructions, adding the fact that this time the eyes must be kept closed.)

*Teacher
Instruction:*   An emphasis should be placed on an awareness of left and right and the change in position of the entire body. Rhythm also should be stressed as well as starting and stopping—starting only after each command has been given and coming to a complete stop after the command has been executed.

Many of the children will display difficulty in maintaining their balance after the command has been executed. It may be necessary to demonstrate and practice the quarter turn before the exercise is begun.

Explanation of the quarter turn is as follows:

The quarter turn takes two counts. On the first count, if you are turning to the left, both feet turn to the left together. The left foot turns with all of the sole in contact with the floor while the right foot turns on the ball of the foot with the heel raised. At this point, the right toe will be just to the right of the left heel. On the second count, the right foot slides up to take a position next to the left foot. (A quarter turn to the right should then be explained.)

Extreme structure and no talking. All commands given in rhythmic manner.

12. TAKE A STANCE

Equipment: Area large enough for children to form two lines with each child facing the teacher and with at least two feet between each child when arms are outstretched.

Objective: Laterality, directionality, rhythm, spacing, sequencing of body movements, auditory memory, starting and stopping, ability to hold a fixed position.

Student Instruction: I want this half of the group (indicate which half) to form a line which will reach from this side of the room to that side of the room and with each of you facing me. Stretch your arms out to the sides of your body and then move apart from one another until there is this much room between each of you (indicate amount of room.)

(The same instruction is then given to the remaining half of the class, after you have turned your back to the first group. This means you will have two rows of children with the rows facing one another.)

I am now going to call out several different commands. The commands will be different things you are to do with your body. First, listen to all of the commands. Then, I will tell you to "take your stance" and I will count as many times as there were commands. If there were two commands, I will count to two. If there were four commands, I will count to four, and so on.

You will hold your stance until I say *"Ready,"* at which time you will return to your original position . . . feet together, hands by your side and your eyes straight ahead.

(At this point, explain that a stance is a particular position you take with your body.)

Remember, each one of you will be looking directly across at another student. Do not try to copy the stance of that student. If you do, your own stance will probably be wrong. Listen to the directions carefully.

Stand up straight, feet together, hands by your side.

1. *Ready*
   Left arm out
   Right leg out
   Take your stance
   One, two.

2. *Ready*
   Right arm out
   Left leg out
   Take your stance
   One, two

3. *Ready*
   Both arms up
   Head to the left
   Right leg back
   Take your stance
   One, two, three

4. *Ready*
   Both arms up
   Head to the right
   Left leg front
   Take your stance
   One, two, three

5. *Ready*
   Both arms out
   Both legs out
   Head to the left
   Bend at the waist
   Take your stance
   One, two, three, four

6. *Ready*
   Left arm out
   Right arm up
   Right leg out
   Head to the left
   Take your stance
   One, two, three, four

Teacher
Instruction: The six groups of commands become progressively harder for the child to execute. It may be necessary to work with only two part commands as in number one and number two for an extended period of time. Under no circumstances should three and four part commands be attempted until two part commands have been mastered.

Difficulty also will be encountered as the children face one another and attempt to execute the same commands. This, however, is an objective of the activity. Each child must develop laterality and directionality in relation to his own body.

In giving the commands, all must be given in a rhythmic manner. The calling of the numbers, when the child is executing the command, should be especially slow as well as rhythmic.

A special emphasis should be placed on the child's awareness of the commands being executed in the manner in which they were called and the development of auditory sequential memory.

Related Reading References

Benyon, Sheila Doran. *Intensive Programming for Slow Learners.* Columbus, Ohio: Charles E. Merrill Publishing Co., 1963, pp. 43-98. An intensified six-week training program aimed at training student teachers for diagnostic teaching in a classroom and providing an atmosphere for structured learning through the utilization of perceptual-motor techniques. Preparations for the establishment of such a program are presented as well as detailed activities used throughout the six-week program at Purdue University.

Chaney, Clara M. and Newell C. Kephart. *Motoric Aids to Perceptual Training.* Columbus, Ohio: Charles E. Merrill Publishing Co., 1968, pp. 3-25, 43-53, 60-63, 79-88, 93-110. A presentation of basic motor and perceptual activities for training children with learning disorders, including the brain injured and retarded.

Child Study Center Publication, *The Foundations of Learning.* Little Rock, Arkansas: University of Arkansas, 1967, pp. 89-148. A comprehensive evaluation of the auditory, visual and motor channels of communication as a basis for the learning process, as well as a compilation of methodology aimed at development of adequate skills in each of these areas. Compiled by the students of Special Education 5316, University of Arkansas Medical Center.

Kephart, Newell C. *The Slow Learner in the Classroom.* 2nd ed. Columbus, Ohio: Charles E. Merrill Publishing Co., 1971, pp. 79-104, 171-183, 209-262. A systematic approach to the identification of slow learner behavior and learning problems including techniques for identifying and correcting specific disabilities.

Teaching through Sensory-Motor Experiences. John I. Arena, ed. San Rafael, California: Academic Therapy Publications, 1969, pp. 35-46, 121-133. A compilation of articles in which the authors, all experienced in working with children, focus on those areas that they have found to be poorly developed or inefficiently and inconsistently integrated in functionally underachieving children. Emphasis is placed on a series of more basic skills which must first develop and become integrated before communication skills are established.

Valett, Robert E. *Programming Learning Disabilities.* Palo Alto, California: Fearon Publishers, 1969, pp. 15-20, 79-82, 93-98, 104-107, 115-122, 153. A practical framework for the actual programming of learning disabilities with an attempt to bridge the gap between existing theory and practice. Covered are the three stages in programming consisting of planning, implementation and remediation.

––––––– "The Remediation of Learning Disabilities" (Tabbed Section of *Gross Motor Development and Sensory Motor Integration*), Palo Alto, California: Fearon Publishers, 1967. A comprehensive and specific program including resource material for children with specific learning disabilities. Six major areas of learning are covered: Gross Motor Development, Sensory-Motor Integration, Perceptual-Motor Skills, Language Development, Conceptual Skills, and Social Skills.

Witsen, Betty Van. *Perceptual Training Activities Handbook.* New York: Teachers College Press, 1967, pp. 51-52, 55-60. A systematically developed and empirically tested group of perceptual training activities designed to be modified and adapted for use in classroom instruction or in tutorials.

chapter 3

1. Color Maze
2. Where Am I
3. Higher or Lower
4. Ball Bounce Change
5. High-Low Ball Bounce
6. Musical Stairs
7. Ball Bounce Echo
8. Stop and Start Walking Cycle
9. Controlled Running
10. Obstacle Course
11. Missing Notes
12. Wings

Auditory Motor Activities

Auditory perception and response is that single act whereby an individual establishes communication with his environment. We recognize, in the realm of communication, the various channels—visual, tactual and kinesthetic—as well as auditory. But that channel through which language develops, matures and becomes most meaningful as it relates to learning and social acceptance is the auditory channel.

Inaccurate perception of that which is taken in auditorily yields an inaccurate auditory motor response. The perception of an auditory stimulus (the intake), therefore, is of initial concern.

Within our framework of communication there are visual, tactual and kinesthetic as well as auditory communications—one often calling the other into effect to produce the appropriate response or motor action.

We will consider tasks wherein a child must make an association between that which is auditorily perceived and the corresponding visual and kinesthetic response. Situations calling for auditory perception of letter and number groupings and the necessary association with the appropriate visual patterns also are to be considered. Auditory-visual discrimination is called forth in the majority of the child's learning situations.

The activities which follow are for the purpose of establishing basic auditory perception motor skills as well as those skills in conjunction with other sensory motor skills called for in specific learning experiences.

Color Maze

1. COLOR MAZE

Equipment: Twenty-eight, five-by-five inch squares cut from red, yel-
                  low, blue, and green oilcloth; seven of each color placed on
                  the floor according to Chapter 6, Diagram 5.

Objective: Auditory awareness and acuity, sequencing, memory span,
                  eye-foot coordination, visual-tactual proficiency.

Student
Instruction: Each of you will line up, one behind the other, behind this
                  line in front of the color maze. We shall try to cross the
                  maze, but first, you will need to listen to the secret combi-
                  nation I shall give to each of you.

                  I shall call out to each of you just before you begin, a
                  combination, or list, of colors; i.e. red, yellow, yellow,
                  green, blue, red, yellow. You must step on these colors, in
                  this order, before you can completely cross the maze.
                  Ready:

Teacher
Instruction: It is not likely that any of the children will be able to remember the sequence of colors you call out on their first attempt; and if you are working with very young children, you will not want to go past a sequence of three or four when first beginning.

Stress listening to the sequence of colors you call out, repeating the sequence aloud before an attempt is made to cross, and eye-foot coordination.

The activity may be varied by placing numbers or letters on the squares and calling out the combination in a number or letter sequence.

Extreme structure and no talking. All commands given in rhythmic manner.

2. WHERE AM I

Equipment: Musical triangle, metal bar.

Objective: Auditory awareness and acuity, attention span.

Student
Instruction: I want all of you to gather in the center of the room, sit down on the floor, close your eyes, and put your heads on your knees. Listen very carefully to everything you hear.

I have in my hand a musical triangle and a metal bar with which to make this sound. (Demonstrate the sound to be made.)

I shall be walking very quietly around the room but you will not know exactly where I am because you will not be able to see me. Then I shall stop and sound the triangle. When you hear the sound, point with your finger and arm in the direction from which you think the sound is coming. When I say, "hands down," put your hands down and I will very quietly move to another position. As soon as you hear the sound again, point to the direction from which you think the sound is coming. *Ready:*

Teacher
Instruction: Stress listening at all times and visualizing in their minds
the striking of the triangle in order that the children may
more readily relate to the sound.

Extreme structure and no talking.

3. HIGHER OR LOWER

Equipment: Piano; area large enough for children to be seated around
the piano with at least three feet between each child.

Objective: Auditory awareness and acuity, attention span, concentration.

Student
Instruction: I want all of you to gather around the piano, on the floor,
with your backs to the piano and your eyes looking toward
the wall. Be sure there is this much space between each of
you. (Indicate amount of space.)

You must be very quiet and listen carefully. I am going to
play a sound on the piano. I shall play the exact same
sound four times in a row. Then I shall play a second
sound, the exact same sound, four times in a row. I shall
then call on one of you to tell me if the second sound I
played was higher or lower than the first sound. You will
not know if it is you I am going to call on or not, so you
must all listen and be ready to answer.

After the first student answers, I shall play another four
sounds, all just alike, and call on another student to tell me
whether it was higher or lower than the last set of sounds
you heard. Listen, and I shall demonstrate. (Demonstrate
with one or two students and then begin.) *Ready:*

Teacher
Instruction: Stress having the complete attention of every child at all
times with each child feeling that he will be called on next.

If auditory perception is very poor, you may need to go up
and down more than just a single note. In some instances

a difference of an entire octave may be necessary before the child is able to discriminate.

Extreme structure and no talking.

4. BALL BOUNCE CHANGE

Equipment: 8½ inch playground ball; piano; area large enough for children to form two lines with at least three feet between each child when arms are outstretched.

Objective: Auditory awareness and acuity, rhythm, change in pitch, eye-hand coordination.

Student
Instruction: I want you to form two lines, down the room, with each of you facing one another. This half of you form one line, and this half, the other line. Spread yourselves out and be sure there is this much space between each of you. (Indicate amount of space.)

We shall begin with this student on the end of this line. I shall begin playing the same sound over and over on the piano. After you have listened a few moments and have decided how fast I am playing, you will begin bouncing the ball in time with the piano. Keep bouncing the ball in time with the piano until you hear me change and begin playing a new sound. When you hear the new sound, you will bounce the ball over to the person in front of you, and he will then begin bouncing in time with the piano. *Ready:*

Teacher
Instruction: Stress listening to the piano and trying to determine the rhythm and time before beginning to bounce the ball. Then stress listening for a change in the sound. Tell the children that sometimes the sound will be lower and sometimes it will be higher and that it is simply a change for which they should be listening.

Extreme structure and no talking.

5. HIGH-LOW BALL BOUNCE

Equipment: 8½-inch playground ball; piano.

Objective: Auditory awareness and acuity, rhythm, high and low, sequencing, eye-hand coordination.

Student
Instruction: Spread yourselves out around the room being sure that you cannot reach out and touch any other person. You will each take your turn in this activity.

I shall start playing a certain note on the piano (the same note over and over). The person whose turn it is first will take the ball and begin bouncing it in time with the piano. As long as I am playing the same note, be sure that you are bouncing the ball the same height every time.

When you hear me change to a different note, listen very carefully. If the sound you hear is higher, you must begin bouncing the ball higher. If the sound you hear is lower, you must begin bouncing the ball lower.

Each time I change, you will change. Start by bouncing the ball about as high as your waist. *Ready:*

Teacher
Instruction: This activity is difficult but creates a great deal of enthusiasm. You will definitely need to demonstrate before the first child attempts the task.

Stress listening and bouncing the ball in time with the piano.

Extreme structure and no talking.

6. MUSICAL STAIRS

Equipment: Stairs constructed according to Chapter 6, Diagram 4; piano.

Objective: Auditory awareness and acuity, left-right progression, sequencing, eye-foot coordination, rhythm, laterality, directionality.

Student
Instruction: I want all of you to line up, one behind the other, at this end of the stairs. We are going to be working on the stairs, one at a time. You must listen very carefully to my instructions and when we begin the activity you must listen just as carefully to the piano. Let's begin with the first student in line.

Step up to the stairs, but not on the stairs. I shall play a sound on the piano and you will step up onto the first step. Then I shall play a second sound on the piano. If the second sound is higher than the first, you will step up on the second step with your right foot; but, if the second sound is lower, you will step back down with your right foot. I may make all of the sounds going up, in which case you will walk right up to the top of the stairs. But, I may go up and then down, and up and then down. You must listen carefully so that you will know which way to step. You also must step slowly because sometimes you will be stepping backwards and you must not begin to step until after you have heard the sound.

Always begin with your left foot and alternate (explain the term "alternation" if necessary) your feet as you go up and down the stairs. *Ready:*

Teacher
Instruction: Stress listening and deciding on the direction before stepping either up or down. Rhythm and alternating feet movements should also be emphasized.

During your instructions to the first student you should demonstrate on the piano what you mean by the sound going higher or lower.

If the children are quite young and unsure of their balance, their hand should be held during the first few attempts.

Extreme structure and no talking.

7. BALL BOUNCE ECHO

Equipment: 8½-inch playground ball; area large enough for children to form a line with each child facing the instructor and with at least two feet between each child.

Objective: Auditory awareness and acuity with and without reinforcement, rhythm.

Student
Instruction: *Part 1.*   I want all of you to form a line with each of you facing me, and with at least this much space between each of you. (Indicate amount of space.) Now that you are in position, you must listen very carefully. I am going to bounce our rubber ball a certain number of times, listen and look. When I stop, I shall call out one of your names, bounce the ball to you, and I shall want you to bounce the ball exactly the same number of times. *Ready:* (Each child takes his turn several times.)

                    Part 2.   Now that you have learned to listen and look, and then repeat what you have heard and seen, we are going to try something just a little different.

                    Stay in your exact same line, only this time, turn around so your backs are toward me and your eyes are facing the opposite wall. (Indicate which wall.)

                    I am going to bounce the ball again a certain number of times and this time you will only be able to listen. When I stop, I shall call out one of your names, bounce the ball to you, and I shall want you to bounce the ball exactly the same number of times. You will not know whom I am going to call on next, so you must all listen carefully each time. *Ready:*

Teacher
Instruction: Stress listening at all times and visualizing the bounce of the ball even when sight is not being used.

                    Many students will be able to repeat the correct number of bounces when using both their vision and their hearing. These same students will not be able to repeat the same number of bounces once they are required to rely on their auditory perception alone.

For very young children, ball bouncing practice may first be necessary.

Extreme structure and no talking.

8. STOP AND START WALKING CYCLE

Equipment: Musical triangle, metal bar; area large enough for children to form a circle with at least five feet between each child.

Objective: Auditory awareness and acuity, rhythm, pacing, spacing, coordination, balance, stopping and starting, execution of movement on a given signal.

Student Instruction: I want all of you to form a circle in the middle of the room by joining hands. Now, drop hands and begin stepping backward until there is this much room between each of you. (Indicate amount of room.) Now I want you to turn to your left and look directly at the back of the person in front of you.

Listen carefully and when you hear me strike the triangle once (demonstrate), you will begin walking around in a circle. You will all try to walk about the same rate of speed; about like this. (Demonstrate.) When you hear me strike the triangle twice, you must all stop immediately. Do not move at all, once you hear the two sounds. Then when you hear just one sound again, you may again begin moving around in the circle.

Listen carefully, try to move together, and try to move in rhythm. *Ready:*

Teacher Instruction: All objectives should be stressed with an emphasis on execution of the proper movement at the proper time and a complete absence of movement at the proper time.

The children will have a tendency to continually be moving their circle in toward the center, thus making it smaller and smaller. It may be necessary to draw a chalk circle on the floor as a pattern for the children to follow.

Extreme structure and no talking.

Under no circumstances should this activity be made competitive as in the case of some games and activities where children are eliminated if they fail to stop or start at the proper time.

9. CONTROLLED RUNNING

Equipment: Space enough for children to form a circle with at least five feet between each child.

Objective: Auditory awareness and acuity, rhythm, spacing, pacing, coordination, balance, body control.

Student
Instruction: I want all of you to form a circle in the middle of the room by joining hands. Now drop hands and begin stepping backward until there is this much room between each of you. (Indicate amount of room.) Now I want you to turn to your left and look directly at the back of the person in front of you.

I am going to begin counting very slowly: 1, 2, 3, 4, over and over. When I feel that you have the rhythm of my counting, I shall raise my hand high in the air. When you see my hand go up, you will start walking around in the circle in time with my counting.

As you are walking, my counting will become faster and faster. The faster I count, the faster you will walk until finally you will be running.

You must listen carefully because as you are running very fast, I shall begin to slow down my counting. You must slow down your running so that finally we shall be walking again.

I shall count fast and then slow, fast and then slow, and you must try to walk and run in rhythm with my counting. *Ready:*

Teacher Instruction: All objectives should be stressed with an emphasis on listening and immediately responding to the rhythm of the counting.

Spacing will be difficult as some of the children will immediately respond to the change in pace while others will not discriminate sufficiently and will continue at the previous pace. It may therefore be necessary to stop on occasion, respace and once again establish the pace.

Extreme structure and no talking.

10. OBSTACLE COURSE

Equipment: Two Indian clubs, one three-foot length of rope, one nine-by-nine inch cardboard square, one nine-inch-diameter cardboard circle, one nine-by-fifteen inch cardboard rectangle, one rocking board. All items arranged according to Chapter 6, Diagram 6.

Objective: Auditory perception, attention span, memory span, sequencing, eye-foot coordination, body control.

Student Instruction: I want all of you to form a line, one behind the other here in front of the line of different objects you see. In order to reach the end of the maze, however, you must listen very carefully to my instructions.

At first I shall give you only one instruction. i.e., "Jump over the Indian club and return to the end of the line." I will be giving each of you a different first instruction so you will not be able to simply follow the student in front of you.

After each of you has done this I shall give you two instructions, i.e. "Jump over the Indian club; step on the square." Once again I shall be giving each of you a different set of instructions so you will not be able to simply follow the student in front of you.

There are seven objects in the obstacle course and I shall continue giving you your instructions, one more instruction each time it is your turn, until you have completely crossed the obstacle course. But remember, you must follow each instruction just as I give it. If you miss one, then you stop where you missed and return to the end of the line to wait for another turn. *Ready:*

*Teacher
Instruction:* Stress listening and visualizing a picture of the correct way to cross the obstacle course as the verbal instructions are given.

Instructions must be changed for each child to prevent the child from visually copying the child just in front of him and to prevent memorizing the pattern of instructions.

An example of a set of all seven commands might be:

1. Jump over the Indian club.

2. Step on the square.

3. Hop over the rope.

4. Go to the left of the circle.

5. Go to the right of the rectangle.

6. Hop over the Indian club.

7. Step onto the rocking board and rock four times.

Extreme structure and no talking.

11. MISSING NOTES

Equipment: Piano; area large enough for children to be seated around the piano with at least three feet between each child.

Objective: Auditory awareness and acuity, attention span, concentration, auditory sequencing, part and part-whole auditory relationships.

Student
Instruction:

I want all of you to gather around the piano, on the floor, with your backs to the piano and your eyes looking toward the wall. Be sure there is this much space between each of you. (Indicate amount of space.)

You must be very quiet and listen carefully. I am going to play four different sounds on the piano. The sounds will be made by four of the keys, all side by side. Listen as I play the four sounds. (Demonstrate.)

Now we are going to give a number name to each of these sounds . . . one, two, three and four. As I play the sounds over several times, let's say their names together and in rhythm. (Demonstrate until the children are calling the notes by their number names together and in rhythm.)

Stop. Now we are ready to see if you can find the missing note.

I will play the four different sounds and I will play them, as a group, three times. As I play them, you will say their number names to yourself . . . not aloud. The fourth time I play them, I will leave out one of the sounds. Then I will stop. When I stop, I want you to raise your hand if you can tell me the number name of the missing sound. Remember, number one is the lowest sound, number four is the highest sound and numbers two and three are in the middle. *Ready:*

Teacher
Instruction:

Stress having complete quiet with each child thinking and hearing and naming each note as it is sounded on the piano.

This is a difficult activity for nearly all perceptually-handicapped children. It may be necessary to begin with only two notes, working gradually up to the sequence of four.

An emphasis also should be placed on hearing each part as it is related to the whole and on auditory sequencing of the sounds as they stair-step from low to high.

Extreme structure and no talking.

12. WINGS

Equipment: Piano; area large enough for children to form a circle with at least six feet between each child.

Objective: Auditory awareness and acuity, rhythm, spacing, pacing, concentration, relationship of body position to auditory intake.

Student
Instruction: I want all of you to form a circle in the middle of the room by joining hands. Now, drop hands and begin stepping backward until there is this much room between each of you. (Indicate amount of room.)

I am going to play three different sounds on the piano. One will be very low, one will be very high and one will be right in the middle. Listen while I play these sounds several times for you. (Demonstrate.)

Your arms are going to be your wings. When I play the very low sound, your wings will be straight down by your sides. When I play the very high sound, your wings will be stretched high above your head. When I play the middle sound, your wings will be stretched straight out to the sides.

I will play each sound eight times. I may first play the high sound, then the low sound, then the middle sound and then the high sound again. The sounds will not be in any certain order.

When I begin playing, you will begin walking around in your circle, following the student just in front of you and looking directly at the back of his head. Walk in rhythm, taking a step every time you hear a sound from the piano.

Remember, you will hear each sound eight times before you hear a different sound. Put your wings in the position in which the sound tells you to place them . . . high, low or in the middle and to the sides. *Ready:*

Teacher
Instruction: This activity calls for a number of different responses from the child and a great deal of concentration and organization. The spacing and pacing of the movement in the circle will be difficult enough and, at the same time, the child will be attempting to relate the position of the sound which is heard to the correct body position.

If too much difficulty is encountered, it first may be necessary to simply place the children in two straight lines and concentrate only on the body positions as related to the sound which is heard. Once this is mastered, the circle formation and marching once again may be attempted.

Extreme structure and no talking

Related Reading References

Chaney, Clara M. and Newell C. Kephart. *Motoric Aids to Perceptual Training.* Columbus, Ohio: Charles E. Merrill Publishing Co., 1968, pp. 67-76. A presentation of the basic motor and perceptual activities for training children with learning disorders, including the brain injured and retarded.

Child Study Center Publication. *The Foundations of Learning.* Little Rock, Arkansas: University of Arkansas, 1967, pp. 1-48. A comprehensive evaluation of the auditory, visual and motor channels of communication as a basis for the learning process—as well as a compilation of methodology aimed at development of adequate skills in each of these areas. Compiled by the students of Special Education 5316, University of Arkansas Medical Center.

Cratty, Bryant J., and Sister Margaret Mary Martin. *Perceptual-Motor Efficiency in Children.* Philadelphia: Lea & Febiger, 1969, pp. 146-155. A program for the development of perceptual-motor efficiency based on principles of child development with an emphasis on the importance of motivating children to learn and the use of movement activities as an aid to learning.

Gearheart, Bill R., and Ernest P. Willenberg. *Application of Pupil Assessment Information: for the Special Education Teacher.* Denver, Colorado: Love Publishing Co., 1970, p. 37. A precise presentation intended: (1) to describe the types, purposes and appropriateness of various testing and evaluative tools and techniques, and to discuss certain educational and psychological terms in common use in our schools; (2) to delve into the role which a classroom teacher should play in this interaction.

Kephart, Newell C. *The Slow Learner in the Classroom.* 2nd ed. Columbus, Ohio: Charles E. Merrill Publishing Co., 1971, pp. 260-262. A systematic approach to the identification of slow learner behavior and learning problems including techniques for identifying and correcting specific disabilities.

Teaching through Sensory-Motor Experiences. John I. Arena, ed. San Rafael, California: Academic Therapy Publications, 1969, pp. 95-103. A compilation of articles in which the authors, all experienced in working with children, focus on those areas that they have found to be poorly developed or inefficiently and inconsistently integrated in functionally underachieving children. Emphasis is placed on a series of basic skills which must first develop and become integrated before communication skills are established.

Valett, Robert E. *Programming Learning Disabilities.* Palo Alto, California: Fearon Publishers, 1969, pp. 20-21, 77, 79, 93, 105, 119-120, 163. A practical framework for the actual programming of learning disabilities with an attempt at bridging the gap between existing theory and practice. Covered are the three stages in programming consisting of planning, implementation and remediation.

————— "The Remediation of Learning Disabilities" (Tabbed Section of *Perceptual Motor Skills*), Palo Alto, California: Fearon Publishers, 1967. A comprehensive and specific program including resource material for children with specific learning disabilities. Six major areas of learning are covered: Gross Motor Development, Sensory-Motor Integration, Perceptual-Motor Skills, Language Development, Conceptual Skills, and Social Skills.

Witsen, Betty Van. *Perceptual Training Activities Handbook.* New York: Teachers College Press, 1967, pp. 30-50. A systematically developed and empirically tested group of perceptual training activities designed to be modified and adapted for use in classroom instruction or in tutorials.

chapter 4

1. The Walking Stumps
2. Jump the Target
3. Swinging Ball Activity #1
4. Swinging Ball Activity #2
5. Swinging Ball Activity #3
6. Swinging Ball Activity #4
7. Ready, Aim, Fire
8. Follow The Beam
9. Visual Tracking and Steering Charts
10. Head and Body Rotations
11. Number Maze
12. Walking Paths and Walking Board

Ocular Motor Activities

Ocular perception is the product of the interaction of all the ocular or visual apparatus and one or more of the remaining sensory modalities resulting in the appropriate motor response. The actual perceiving or taking in of that which is in our environment through the ocular apparatus assumes that an individual first has been exposed to a situation and that the necessary ocular motor skills have been sufficiently established. It then follows that interpretation and conceptualization will produce an appropriate learned motor response. An inadequate visual motor match results in an inappropriate or distorted response.

Just as we recognize that auditory communication often calls into effect other sensory channels of communication in order that the appropriate motor response will be produced, so do we recognize that visual communication often calls upon the auditory, tactual and kinesthetic sensory modalities in order that communication and appropriate response may take place.

In this respect, consideration may first be given to the copying of letter, number or form configurations. This task not only calls for adequate visual perception in the form of visual perception memory, visual sequencing, visual conceptualization of pattern and form and visual discrimination, but also visual perception in association with the correct kinesthetic response.

The ocular motor activities which follow are designed to develop not only the basic ocular perception skills, per se, but the ocular perception skills in association with one or all of the remaining sensory modalities called for in specific learning situations.

Walking Stumps

1. THE WALKING STUMPS

Equipment: Ten blocks of wood, each with a 12" base and a 12" surface top, varying in height from 4" to 18", placed on the floor in a vertical line according to Chapter 6, Diagram 7.

Objective: Visual awareness and acuity, visual steering, depth perception, eye-foot coordination, balance, visual-tactual proficiency.

Student Instruction: Each of you will line up, one behind the other, behind this line. We are going to try to cross another maze, only this time it is a maze of tree stumps.

Only one of you will attempt to cross at a time. Some of the time you will need to step up and some of the time you will need to step down. Use your eyes as well as your feet to guide you across. *Ready:*

Teacher
Instruction: All of the objectives of this activity should be stressed, emphasizing looking and seeing before stepping to a different level.

If the child is unsure and his balance is poor, his hand should be held during the first few attempts.

Extreme structure and no talking.

2. JUMP THE TARGET

Equipment: Two parallel lines, 14' in length, 10" apart, constructed of ½" colored tape, and marked at the mid-point. One 8½" rubber playground ball.

Objective: Visual awareness and acuity, precision, ability to visually judge and perceive motion and speed, body control, coordination.

Student
Instruction: I want all of you to line up at this end of the parallel lines, one behind the other with at least three feet of space between each of you. (Indicate amount of space.) I shall be at the other end of the parallel lines and shall be holding our rubber playground ball.

I want the first student in line to step up to the mid-point of the parallel lines, where you see the "X." Face me, with your side next to the parallel lines, and as close to the parallel lines as you can be without being on them.

I am going to roll the ball down between the two lines. Look at the ball coming toward you and try to decide when it will be right by your side. When you have jumped to the other side, turn around and face the line of students, keeping your body just as close to the parallel lines as you can without being on them.

The student who is now first in line will have caught the ball and will roll it back to me. You will have two chances each time it is your turn, so try once again to jump the ball just as it rolls over the mid-point.

After you have had your two chances, go to the end of the
line of students. The student now first in line will take his
place at the mid-point of the parallel lines.

Try to time your jumping; not too soon and not too late.
Jump high enough so as not to hit the ball and immediately
turn around for your second try. *Ready:*

*Teacher
Instruction:*   Stress acquiring the ability to visually judge and perceive
motion and speed. Emphasize also the simultaneous mo-
tions: the body going over the ball as the ball passes
beneath the body.

Do not allow the children to face the parallel lines in
jumping over the ball. The side of the body must be placed
next to the lines at all times, with the child facing the
direction from which the ball is being rolled.

Extreme structure and no talking.

3. SWINGING BALL ACTIVITY #1

Equipment: Swinging ball attached to the ceiling so that it can be raised
and lowered; flash cards. See Chapter 6, Diagram 8 for
construction of ball and flash cards.

Objective: Peripheral awareness and peripheral acuity, visual tracking, visual steering, visual awareness and acuity.

*Student
Instruction:*   You will form a line, one behind the other, behind the
swinging ball, with at least three feet of space between each
of you. (Indicate amount of space.)

I want the first student in line to lie down on the floor with
your eyes directly under the ball. I shall put the ball in
motion swinging from side to side across your eyes.

Straighten your body, hands by your side, feet together.
Keep your head and shoulders perfectly still and let only
your eyes follow the ball from side to side. *Ready:*

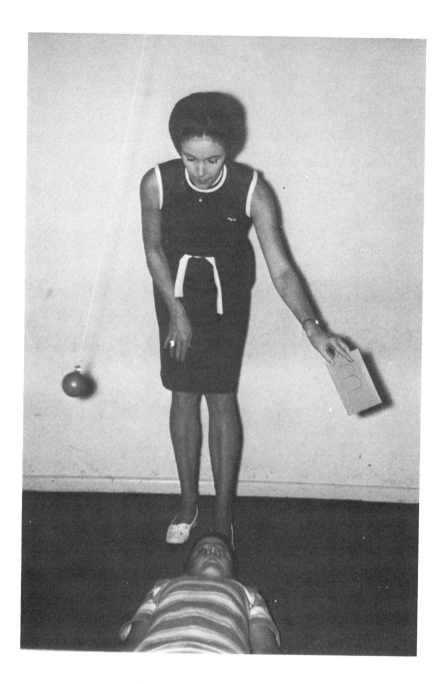

Swinging Ball Activity # 1

(After this has been established . . .) Now, as your eyes are following the ball, I am going to flash a card on one side or the other of your eyes. The card will have a number on it, and without taking your eyes off the ball, I want you to tell me the number you saw. *Ready:*

Teacher Instruction: Each objective should be stressed and no child should work on each of the phases of this activity for more than a minute at a time. (Even this will be too long for some children.)

When flashing the card, you should stand directly behind the child. Flash the card to the left when the child is following the ball to the right and to the right when the child is following the ball to the left. Card should be flashed out for no longer than a second.

The same procedure should be followed in varying the activity in the following manner: ball swinging in direction from head to toe, ball swinging in a circular direction.

Extreme structure and no talking.

4. SWINGING BALL ACTIVITY #2

Equipment: Swinging ball attached to the ceiling so that it can be raised and lowered. Small red rubber ball 1½" in diameter on the end of a 3' dowel, ¼" in diameter. See Chapter 6, Diagram 8 for construction.

Objective: Visual awareness and acuity, visual steering, visual tracking, visual movement with body fixation.

Student Instruction: I want all of you to form a line, one behind the other, here in front of the swinging ball. You will each take your turn, one at a time.

When it is your turn, you will take the stick with the red ball on the end in your hand. I shall start the ball swinging and, as I do, you will try to follow the swinging ball when

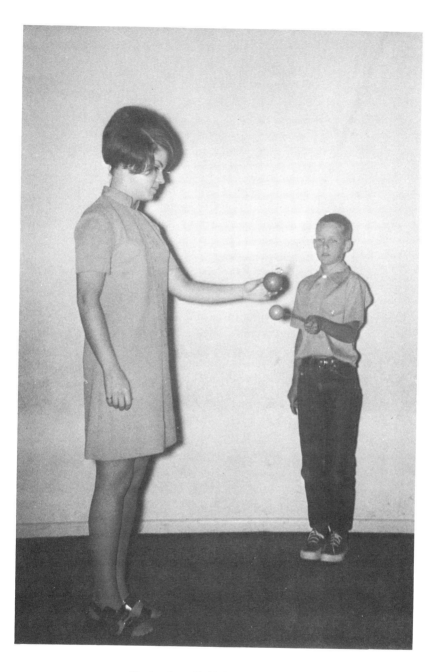

Swinging Ball Activity #2

it goes one way, and you will try to lead the swinging ball when it goes the other way. You must try to get the little red ball as close to the swinging ball as you can without touching it. I shall first show you what I mean. (Demonstrate.)

This may be difficult for you at first because you must watch two objects at the same time: the small red ball on the end of your stick and the larger swinging ball.

Remember also that we are going to use only our eyes to tell us what to do. I shall want you to hold your shoulders and your head very still and move only your eyes. I shall help each of you begin by standing in front of you and guiding the red ball with my hand until you have the feel of the motion. *Ready:*

Teacher
Instruction: Stress keeping the red ball as close to the swinging ball as possible without touching it, with a special emphasis on keeping the head and shoulders still and moving only the eyes.

If a visual perception deficit exists, this activity will be difficult. It may also be a very tiring exercise and should not be attempted for too long a period of time. (Thirty seconds should be sufficient each time the child has a new turn.)

Note the child's ability to move both eyes in a rhythmic manner from the extreme left to the extreme right without jerking or hesitating. Especially note any inability to cross the midline.

Extreme structure and no talking.

5. SWINGING BALL ACTIVITY #3

Equipment: Swinging ball attached to the ceiling so that it can be raised and lowered. See Chapter 6, Diagram 8 for construction.

Objective: Visual motor response, visual awareness, visual acuity, visual tracking, depth perception, rhythm of movement, ability to judge and perceive motion and speed.

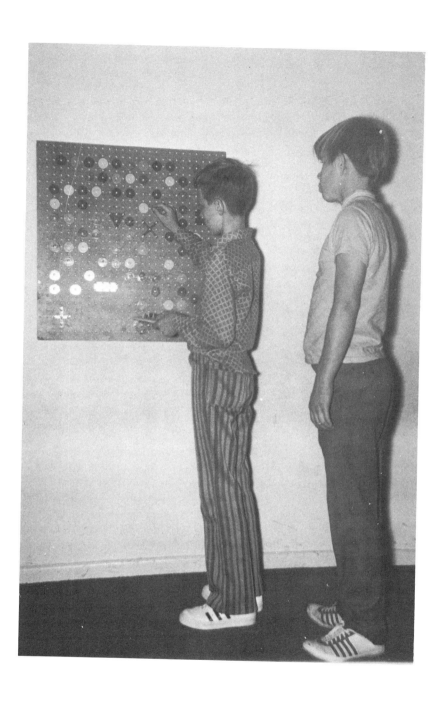

Ready, Aim, Fire

61

*Student
Instruction:*   I want all of you to form a line, one behind the other, here in front of the swinging ball. You will each take your turn, one at a time.

When it is your turn, you will take your position directly behind the swinging ball, facing the other students who will remain in line, and perform the activity. Then you will return to the end of the line while the second student in line takes his turn.

(Take the first student in line and demonstrate as you give the following directions.)

Take your position directly behind the swinging ball, so close that your head is touching the ball. Now, as I stand facing you, I am going to take the ball and pull it straight out from you and as far away from you as I can. When I say *Ready,* I am going to let the ball go and it will swing back toward you, aimed directly at your head.

As it approaches your head, I will call *Dodge.* At this point, you will bend your head to the left in order to let the ball go by on your right side. Then, while the ball is behind you, you will bend your head to the right in order to let the ball return on your left side. You will repeat these actions as long as the ball is swinging high enough and until I say *Stop.*

Remember that you must not take your eyes off the ball as it begins to swing toward you. Remember also that you just must imagine being able to see the ball while it is in back of you. Do not duck your body to avoid being hit by the ball . . . bend it to one side and then the other. *Ready:*

*Teacher
Instruction:*   There are many skills involved in this activity and it is important that it be carried out with precision. The children probably will be apprehensive upon their first attempt. It may be necessary, therefore, to control the ball with your hand in slow-motion fashion in order to let them first get the feel of having the ball move toward them.

The children quite naturally will bend their bodies out of the way of the ball sooner than is necessary in order to avoid being hit. As they become more familiar with the skills involved, an emphasis should be placed on movement just seconds before the ball approaches their heads.

Stress bending the body to the left and to the right rather than squatting down to avoid being hit and bending just enough rather than an excessive amount.

Vary the activity by having the children bend first to the left as the ball is directed toward them and, on other occasions, to the right as the ball is directed toward them.

Extreme structure and no talking.

6. SWINGING BALL ACTIVITY #4

Equipment: Swinging ball attached to the ceiling in a way so that it can be raised and lowered. See Chapter 6, Diagram 8 for construction.

Objective: Eye-hand coordination, visual awareness, visual acuity, visual steering, visual tracking, visual fixation, visual motor match.

*Student
Instruction:* I want all of you to form a line, one behind the other, here in front of the swinging ball. You each will take your turn, one at a time.

When it is your turn, you will take your position one foot (indicate this amount of space) directly behind the swinging ball, facing the other students who will remain in line, and perform the activity. Then you will return to the end of the line while the second student in line takes his turn.

(Take the first student in line and demonstrate as you give the following directions.)

Take your position directly behind the swinging ball as you were instructed. (Place the child if he is not approximately one foot away from the ball, and raise or lower the ball until it is exactly chest-high on the child.)

Raise your hands in front of you, chest-high, between yourself and the ball. Your hands should be layered, left hand on top of the right hand, slightly apart and with both palms down in karate fashion (flat part down). Raise your elbows until they are level with your hands, stiffen your arms and hands and hold this position throughout the activity.

Now you are ready to begin. Strike the ball, gently, with the outer edge of your left hand. Then bring the left hand back, down and under the right hand. This leaves your right hand now on top and ready to strike the ball. This process is then repeated, again and again until I tell you to stop.

Remember that the purpose is to hit the ball each time it swings back toward you, in rhythm, and you should try to make it swing out the same distance from you each time. Do not try to see how far out you can hit it. This is not important.

Remember, too, that your eyes and hands must work together. Keep your eyes on the ball at all times and not on your hands. *Ready:*

*Teacher
Instruction:*   Eye-hand coordination and the ability to judge and perceive motion and speed should be stressed. An emphasis also should be placed on the eyes being visually fixed upon the ball rather than the hands.

This will be difficult for some children because of the fear of being hit by the ball. Manual control of the ball by the instructor may, therefore, be necessary in the initial stages of the activity.

This is a stimulating activity, especially for the boys who will take on the role of one involved in karate. Extreme structure and no talking should, therefore, be encouraged.

7. READY, AIM, FIRE

Equipment: Pegboard constructed according to Chapter 6, Diagram 9. Pegs sufficient in number for children in class.

Objective: Visual awareness and acuity, visual steering, visual tracking, motor movement on visual command as well as auditory command, eye-hand coordination.

*Student
Instruction:* I want all of you to form a line, one behind the other, here in front of the pegboard, with at least three feet between each of you. (Indicate amount of room.) You will each take your turn one at a time.

In front of you on the wall is the pegboard. Each little hole on the board and a one-eighth inch area surrounding the hole has been painted a different color, either red, blue, green, or yellow. Attached to the wall just below the board is a box full of pegs, also colored red, blue, green, and yellow.

I want the first student in line to step up to the line on the floor in front of the pegboard and stand very still with your hands by your side and your eyes looking toward me. When I say *Ready,* you will reach into the box and choose a colored peg, any color, and keep your eyes on the peg you choose. When I say *Aim,* you will draw your arm back and aim with your eyes toward one of the holes on the board which is the same color as the peg you have chosen. When I say *Fire,* you will direct the peg into the proper hole. Let me have the first student demonstrate. (Demonstrate until the children are aware of the procedure.)

*Teacher
Instruction:* All objectives should be stressed with an emphasis on immediate response to your auditory command and a motor response as a result of their own visual command.

Extreme structure and no talking.

8. FOLLOW THE BEAM

Equipment: Flashlight with a strong beam which will make a vivid spotting on the wall. Wall area large enough for patterns to be made with beam of light. Area should accommodate patterns up to six feet by six feet in size.

Objective: Visual awareness and acuity, visual steering, visual track-
                        ing, visual motor movement without verbal reinforcement,
                        rhythm of movement.

*Student
Instruction:*   I want all of you to form a line, one behind the other, with
                        the first student standing just behind this line I have placed
                        on the floor, and with at least three feet of space between
                        each of you. (Indicate amount of space.)

                        I have darkened the room just a little and we are going to
                        be working with patterns made with a flashlight and seen
                        on the wall in front of you.

                        When we begin, I shall turn on the flashlight and fix the
                        beam in a certain position on the wall. I shall want the first
                        student in line to look steadily at the point of light I am
                        making on the wall. As I begin to move the point of light
                        around over the wall, I want you to follow the point of
                        light with your eyes. Use only your eyes and do not move
                        your bodies.

                        At first I shall simply move the point of light from place
                        to place on the wall and you will follow it with your eyes.
                        After each of you has mastered this procedure, I shall
                        begin to make patterns on the wall with the point of light
                        as it becomes your turn. After I have completed the pat-
                        tern for each of you, I shall ask you to name the pattern
                        I made with the flashlight and the pattern you made with
                        your eyes. It may be a square, or a circle, or a triangle, or
                        any number of other patterns. *Ready:*

*Teacher
Instruction:*   Stress keeping the body perfectly still, especially the head
                        and shoulders, and following the light only with the eyes.

                        The room will only be dimmed, not completely dark. You
                        will therefore be able to note the eye movements of each
                        child. You should especially be aware of the smoothness
                        and rhythm of each movement and the precision with
                        which a directional change in eye movement is made.

The movements made with the flashlight and the speed with which directional changes of the light take place will depend upon the individual child. If the visual deficit is such that following the beam is extremely difficult for any one child, the movements of the light should then be made very slowly and in patterns requiring very simple eye movements.

Once the children have learned to track the light and you begin on patterns, you should try all of the following:

1. Square
2. Circle
3. Triangle
4. Rectangle
5. Cross (turn light off after making the first line and then on again to make the second line)
6. X (turn light off after making the first line and then on again to make the second line)
7. Letters, block (turn light off and on as necessary in order to show only the actual lines of the letters)
8. Numbers (turn light off and on as necessary in order to show only the actual lines of the numbers)
9. Letters, cursive (turn light off and on as necessary in order to show only the actual lines of the letters)

Extreme structure and no talking.

9. VISUAL TRACKING AND STEERING CHARTS

Equipment: Three charts constructed according to Chapter 6, Diagram 10, and placed on wall.

Objectives: Visual tracking, visual steering, visual-tactual proficiency, rhythm of movement, visual awareness and acuity, eye-hand coordination.

Student Instruction: I am going to divide the class into three as nearly equal groups as possible and give each group a number. (Divide

groups and number.) Now I want Group 1 to line up, one
behind the other, in front of Chart 1; Group 2, in front of
Chart 2; and Group 3, in front of Chart 3. Three of you
will be working on the charts at the same time; but not
until you have heard the instructions.

On Chart 1 you see four little birds with paths leading to
their own little houses. The birds are colored red, blue,
green and yellow. If you look very carefully, you will see
that the path of the red bird leads to the red house. (Demonstrate by tracking the path of the red bird, with your
finger, to the red house. Then demonstrate with each of the
other colored birds on Chart 1.)

On Chart 2 you see four flowers, each with a path leading
to the pot in which it should be planted. On Chart 3 you
see four socks with a path leading to the matching sock
which will make them a pair. On all three charts the color
of either the birdhouse, the flower pot, or the other sock
will tell you if you have followed the correct path.

Part 1.   Now I want the first student in each line to walk
up to the chart. Place your finger on either a bird, a flower,
or a sock, and try to follow the path with your finger to
either the birdhouse, the flower pot, or the other sock. If
you miss the first time, try at least two more times to follow
the correct path and then let the next student in line have
his turn. *Ready:* (Each child takes his turn.)

Part 2.   Now that you have all tried this part of the
activity, we are going to try something a little more difficult. This time you will also try to follow the correct path
from one object to another, but you must not use your
finger in following the path. You must use only your eyes.
When you have followed the path to the end with your eyes
only, put your finger on the object you have reached, look
back to where you began and see if you followed the correct path. Do the colors match?

If you miss the first time, try at least two more times to
follow the correct path with your eyes and then let the next
student in line have his turn. *Ready:* (Each child takes his
turn.)

Teacher
Instruction: All objectives should be stressed with an emphasis on rhythm of hand and eye movements and then on eye movements alone.

With three groups working at the same time, you will be constantly moving from one group to another to be assured that proper procedure is being carried out.

Caution the child not to hurry and to try to move slowly along the path. Also see that the child chooses a different object to follow each time he has a turn in order to avoid rote learning.

After each child in each group has had a turn at a given chart, rotate the groups.

Extreme structure and no talking.

10. HEAD AND BODY ROTATIONS

Equipment: Four red cardboard squares six-by-six inches in size.

Objective: Visual fixation with body or body parts in motion, balance, coordination, flexibility, laterality, directionality.

Student
Instruction: I am going to divide the class into four groups as nearly equal as possible and I shall place each group in front of one of the red squares you see on the wall. (Place each group to enable each child to clearly see one of the red squares.)

There are several parts to this activity but there is one thing you must always do, even during my instruction and while we are changing from one activity to the next. You must always keep your eyes on the red square in front of your group. *Ready:*

Part 1. Stand up very straight and bend your head as far forward as possible, still keeping your eyes on the red square. Now begin to roll your head around on your shoulders: to the left, to the back, to the right, and back around to the front again. Keep your eyes always on the red square and continue doing this until I tell you to stop.

Part 2.   Stand up very straight and bend your body sideways as far to the left as possible and then sideways as far to the right as possible. Remember to keep your eyes on the red square and continue doing this, from side to side, until I tell you to stop.

Part 3.   Sit down on the floor with your feet together, hands in your lap, your backs very straight, and your eyes still on the red square. Now, bend forward from your waist as far as possible and begin to roll your body, just as you did your head, to the left, to the back, to the right, and back around to the front. Keep your eyes on the red square and continue doing this until I tell you to stop.

Teacher Instruction: All objectives should be stressed with a special emphasis on continual visual fixation.

It is necessary that you place the groups carefully enabling each child to have sufficient space in which to perform each part of the activity.

Encourage slow and rhythmic body movements in that this better enables the child to hold his fixation point.

Extreme structure and no talking.

11. NUMBER MAZE

Equipment: Twenty-eight five-by-five inch squares cut from yellow oilcloth, each with a number printed on the square. Red five-by-five inch cardboard square. For placement see Chapter 6, Diagram 11.

Objective: Visual awareness and acuity, visual-tactual proficiency, eye-foot coordination, rhythm, sequencing, visual and motor response on command.

Student
Instruction: Each of you will line up, one behind the other, behind this line in front of the number maze. We shall each try to cross the maze, but first, you will need to listen to my instructions.

When the first student in line is ready to begin, I want him to step up to this line and look directly ahead of himself at the red cardboard square on the wall. (Indicate wall and cardboard square.) Do not look down at the numbered squares on the floor.

I shall call out a number and I shall want you to do three things: *Think, Look,* and *Step. Think* about the number I call, still keeping your eyes on the red square; *Look* at the numbered squares on the floor and find the one in the first row which I called; and *Step* on that square. *Think, Look,* and *Step.* Did you hear how I said this in rhythm? This is how I want you to move across the maze . . . in rhythm.

Just as soon as you have stepped on the first number I call out, I shall call out a second number in the second row. You will do just as you did after I called out the first number. Remember, you must keep your eyes on the red square on the wall in front of you until after you have heard the number I call. After you have stepped on the number I called, return your eyes to the red square and wait for the next number to be called.

Each of you will take your turn and after you have crossed the maze return to the end of the line and wait for your next turn.

Teacher
Instruction: Special emphasis should be placed on rhythm, visual and motor response on command, and keeping a visual fixation until ready to move.

The numbers on the squares will run from one to twenty-four. There will, however, be a one, a two, or a three in every row for those children who do not as yet know their numbers well.

Extreme structure and no talking.

Walking Paths and Walking Board

12. WALKING PATHS AND WALKING BOARD

Equipment: Three walking paths, each 14' in length, constructed of green oilcloth: path #1, 14" in width; path #2, 10" in width; path #3, 6" in width; walking board; wand; four 8½-inch rubber playground balls. For construction and placement see Chapter 6, Diagram 12.

Objective: Balance, laterality, directionality, visual direction of movement, body coordination, eye-foot coordination, depth perception, left-right progression.

Student
Instruction: We are going to work now on the paths and on the walking board. Here you see the three paths: the first path wider than the second path, and the second path wider than the third path. After the third path you see the walking board.

I want all of you to line up here, one behind the other, at this end of the widest walking path. Each day when we come to this activity, this is where, and how, you will line up. In every part of the activity we shall always do the activity first by going down path #1, coming back up path #2, going down path #3, and finally coming back up on the walking board.

You will be following one another. When the second student in line sees the first student step off path #1, he may begin; when the third student in line sees the second student step off path #1, he may then begin; and so on until the last student comes off the walking board. Then we are ready to begin a new part of the activity. Always begin on your left foot.

Part 1. Choose any way you would like to walk: big steps, little steps, or heel-to-toe fashion. Watch your feet as you walk and travel all three paths and the walking board.

Part 2. This time I want each of you to walk on the paths and the walking board heel-to-toe fashion keeping your eyes fixed on the red dot on the end of the path or the board on which you are walking. Do not look at your feet. You are in your stocking feet and by feeling the slick oilcloth beneath your feet, you can tell whether or not you are still walking on the path. Feel the toes of one foot with the heel of the other as you place your feet, one in front of the other.

Part 3. As you begin your walk this time, I want you to fix your eyes on the little red ball on the end of my stick. I shall move the ball along path #1 just about a foot in front of your feet. Again you must feel the oilcloth beneath your feet and feel the toes of one foot with the heel of the other as you place your feet, one in front of the other, heel-to-toe fashion.

I shall use the ball for each of you only on path #1. As you travel the other paths and the board, keep your eyes looking directly in front of you. Do not look at your feet.

Part 4. I shall now stand at the end of path #1 with my stick and little red ball. As you walk heel-to-toe fashion down the path, fix your eyes on the red ball and follow it with your eyes everywhere it goes. As you travel the other paths and board, keep your eyes looking directly in front of you. Do not look at your feet.

Part 5.   Now we are going to begin working with the ball. I shall hand a ball to the first student in line. As you finish the activity and step off the board, hand your ball to the student at the end of the line who will pass it up to the student who will be needing it next. This way, none of you will have to wait for a ball.

Now to begin. Take two heel-to-toe steps, stop, and bounce the ball in the middle of the path or board. You should say to yourselves while you are traveling, "heel-to-toe, heel-to-toe, bounce in the middle." Keep repeating this, as you walk, until you step off the end of the board.

Keep your eyes straight ahead of you while you are walking heel-to-toe and your eyes on the ball when you bounce in the middle.

Part 6.   This will be a little more difficult. First you will walk heel-to-toe, heel-to-toe, bounce in the middle; next, heel-to-toe, heel-to-toe, bounce to the left; and last, heel-to-toe, heel-to-toe, bounce to the right. You will continue repeating this pattern until you step off the walking board.

When you bounce the ball to the left, you will bounce the ball off the path, or off the board. When you bounce the ball to the right, you will also bounce the ball off the path or board. But when you bounce in the middle, you will bounce the ball in the middle of either the path or the board.

Keep your eyes straight ahead of you while you are walking heel-to-toe; keep your eyes on the ball when you are bouncing to the left, to the right, or in the middle.

*Teacher
Instruction:*   All objectives should be stressed with an emphasis on balance and a visual fixation when required.

The activities which can be performed on the paths and on the walking board are many and varied. You will find, after these six parts of the activity have been mastered, that you will be able to invent other activities which will be helpful in emphasizing the objectives of the activity.

You should especially note the following:

1. General balance.
2. Pulling of the body to one side or the other.
3. Inability to stay on the path or the board unless watching the feet.
4. Lack of tactual awareness in walking on the oilcloth paths.
5. Inability to produce a second motor action (bouncing the ball) while maintaining balance on the path or the board.
6. Lack of laterality and lack of directionality.

The paths are very necessary, and regardless of ability, a child should never begin these activities on the board. Even in the child with a very small deficit, there is a certain amount of apprehension, and perhaps fear, when first beginning to walk on the board.

With very young children, or with children manifesting an outstanding motor deficit, it may be that extensive work on only the paths will be necessary for a period of time. The walking board should not be used until the child can achieve at least some degree of success.

Extreme structure and no talking.

Related Reading References

Chaney, Clara M. and Newell C. Kephart. *Motoric Aids to Perceptual Training.* Columbus, Ohio: Charles E. Merrill Publishing Co., 1968, pp. 19-21, 54-59, 71, 113-120. A presentation of the basic motor and perceptual activities for training children with learning disorders, including the brain injured and retarded.

Child Study Center Publication. *The Foundations of Learning.* Little Rock, Arkansas. 1967, pp. 49-88. A comprehensive evaluation of the auditory, visual and motor channels of communication as a basis for the learning process—as well as a compilation of methodology aimed at development of adequate skills in each of these areas. Compiled by the students of Special Education 5316, University of Arknasas Medical Center.

Cratty, Bryant J. and Sister Margaret Mary Martin. *Perceptual-Motor Efficiency in Children.* (Philadelphia: Lea and Febiger, 1969), pp. 50, 98-145, 183-190. A program for the development of perceptual-motor efficiency based on principles of child development with an emphasis on the importance of motivating children to learn and the use of movement activities as an aid to learning.

Frostig, M. and D. Horne. *The Frostig Program for the Development of Visual Perception.* Chicago: Follett Educational Corporation, 1964. A program designed to help train young children in visual perceptual skills. Originally planned for preschool children; however, it is also suitable for kindergarten and first-grade children who have had no previous visual perceptual training.

Gearheart, Bill R. and Ernest P. Willenberg. *Application of Pupil Assessment Information: For the Special Education Teacher.* Denver, Colorado: Love Publishing Co., 1970, pp. 32-36. A precise presentation intended: (1) to describe the types, purposes and appropriateness of various testing and evaluative tools and techniques, and to discuss certain educational and psychological terms in common use in our schools; (2) to delve into the roll which a classroom teacher should play in this interaction.

Kephart, Newell C. *The Slow Learner in the Classroom.* 2nd ed. Columbus, Ohio: Charles E. Merrill Publishing Co., 1971, pp. 123-141, 143-168, 242-259, 265-311, 313-424. A systematic approach to the identification of slow learner behavior and learning problems including techniques for identifying and correcting specific disabilities.

Marsden, C. D. "The Marsden Ball." *Visual Training At Work—Optometric Extension Program Papers,* 25, No. 8, 1953. A survey of the development of visual perception as related to learning and the training process through which development occurs.

Teaching through Sensory-Motor Experiences. John I. Arena, ed. San Rafael, California: Academic Therapy Publications, 1969, pp. 27-34, 63-76, 77-85, 87-93, 108-110. A compilation of articles in which the authors, all experienced in working with children, focus on those areas that they have found to be poorly developed or inefficiently and inconsistently integrated in functionally underachieving children. Emphasis is placed on a series of more basic skills which must first develop and become integrated before communication skills are established.

Valett, Robert E. *Programming Learning Disabilities.* Palo Alto, California: Fearon Publishers, 1969, pp. 21-23, 81-82, 106-107, 120-122. A practical framework for the actual programming of learning disabilities with an attempt at bridging the gap between existing theory and practice. Covered are the three stages in programming consisting of planning, implementation and remediation.

_____ "The Remediation of Learning Disabilities." (Tabbed Section of *Perceptual Motor Skills*). (Palo Alto, California: Fearon Publishers, 1967). A comprehensive and specific program including resource material for children with specific learning disabilities. Six major areas of learning are covered: Gross Motor Development, Sensory-Motor Integration, Perceptual-Motor Skills, Language Development, Conceptual Skills, and Social Skills.

Witsen, Betty Van. *Perceptual Training Activities Handbook.* New York: Teachers College Press, 1967, pp. 11-29. A systematically developed and empirically tested group of perceptual training activities designed to be modified and adapted for use in classroom instruction or in tutorials.

chapter 5

1. Identification of Body Parts
2. Over and Under Space Bar
3. Think and Choose
4. Mountain Climb
5. Positions in Space
6. Growing Trees
7. Rope Throw
8. Mechanical Imitations
9. Jumping Rope
10. Trampoline
11. Space Travel
12. My Shadow

Body and Space Awareness Activities

The one single entity with which a child should first become totally and completely acquainted is his body . . . and his body as related to all other elements as they are synthesized into his total environment. The relationship the child establishes with all environmental factors throughout his lifetime is dependent upon this acquaintance. For it is his body which remains concrete and unchanging as a "unit of measure" for all else.

The tool with which a child first begins the task of environmental exploration is his body. He sees size . . . as it relates to his body. He measures distance . . . as it relates to his body. He observes form . . . as it relates to his body. He becomes aware of all that surrounds him as it correlates with his body image.

The child who develops false concepts relative to his body also will conceive falsely of his environment. From this point, the child continues to view with distortion all sequential and basic learning concepts relative to upward and progressive academic achievement.

The following body and space awareness activities represent some of the basic skills which must be developed to assure an orderly and accurate perception of body and space.

1. IDENTIFICATION OF BODY PARTS

Equipment: Space enough for children to form two lines with each child facing the instructor and with at least two feet between each child when arms are outstretched.

Objective: Body and body parts awareness, body image.

Student
Instruction: I want this half of the group (indicate which half) to form
                      a line with each of you facing me. Stretch your arms out
                      to the sides of your body and then move apart from one
                      another until there is this much room between each of you
                      (indicate amount of room).

                      (The same instruction is then given to the remaining half
                      of the class, having them form their line in front of the first
                      group.)

                      Part 1.   We are going to talk about and think about the
                      different parts of your body. When I tell you to begin, I
                      want you to hold your two index fingers up in front of you.
                      (Indicate which fingers to hold up.) I shall then begin
                      calling out different parts of your body. With your eyes
                      open, but with your eyes looking directly at me, I want you
                      to point, with both fingers, to the parts of your body I call.
                      Ready:

                      1.   To your head
                      2.   To your eyes
                      3.   To your nose
                      4.   To your mouth
                      5.   To your ears
                      6.   To your shoulders
                      7.   To your elbows
                      8.   To your wrists
                      9.   To your hands
                      10. To your fingers
                      11. To your chest
                      12. To your waist
                      13. To your hips
                      14. To your knees
                      15. To your ankles
                      16. To your feet
                      17. To your toes

                      Part 2.   Now we are going to do the exact same thing,
                      only this time we will do it with our eyes closed. *Ready:*

                      (Repeat list of body parts.)

Part 3. Once again we are going to talk about our bodies. This time I want you to lie down on the floor exactly where you are. Hold the same two fingers up and in front of you and point to the body parts I call out. When you come to a part of your body to which you cannot point, pull your body up into a sitting position and then point to the body part. (Demonstrate this procedure as in pointing to the feet and toes and perhaps even the knees.) *Ready:*

(Repeat list of body parts.)

Teacher Instruction:

Stress the individual parts of the body, and then all of these parts making a whole.

In each part of the activity, you should continue calling the sequence of parts until every child knows the procedure and has an idea of at least some of the body parts. Once this has been fairly well established, change your calling sequence and begin to skip around to various parts of the body.

Part 2 will be more difficult than Part 1, and Part 3 will probably be more difficult than Part 2. The children are in a different environment when their eyes are closed and in Part 3 they are working on a different plane. To some of your children, when working on a different plane, up will no longer be up, and down will no longer be down, etc. This laterality and directionality confusion will affect their conception of where their body parts actually are.

Extreme structure and no talking. All commands given in a rhythmic manner.

2. OVER AND UNDER SPACE BAR

Equipment:

Over-and-under-space-bar constructed according to Chapter 6, Diagram 13.

Objective:

Space awareness, body position and awareness, coordination, body control, judging, estimating.

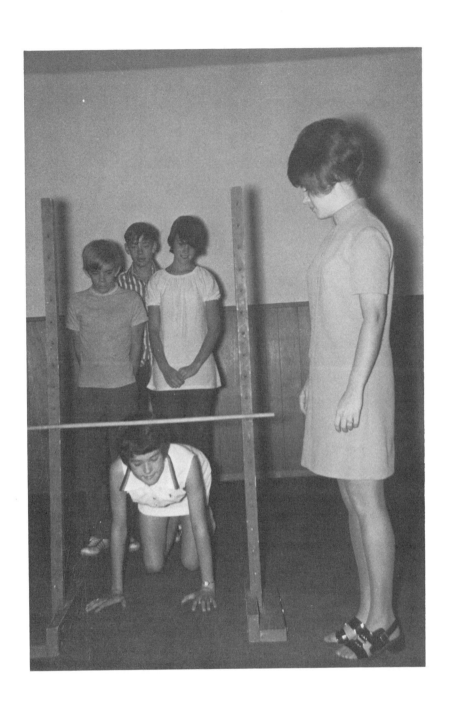

Over and Under Space Bar

Student
Instruction: *Part 1.*   I want the entire group to line up, one behind the other, behind the space bar. (Bar is placed on very top rungs.) First we are going to talk. Tell me what this is between the top bar and the floor, and the sides of the space bar. (The answer is space.) Yes, it is space. Now I want each of you to take your bodies and walk through the space and around to the end of the line.

Now I am going to lower the bar at the top. What has happened to the space? (The answer is that the space has become smaller.) Yes, the space has become smaller. Now, if you come through again and the space is smaller, what will you need to do with your bodies? (The answer is to make their bodies smaller.) Yes, so make your bodies smaller and walk through the space around to the end of the line. *Ready:*

(The space is continually made smaller until the children must move through on their stomachs.)

Part 2.   This time we are going to start by placing the bar on the very lowest rung of the stand. The first student will start on the green line which is 12 ft. away from the bar. First I want you to stand still and simply look at the bar. Think about how far away it is from you and how many steps it will take for you to reach the bar.

Still standing still, next think about how high the bar is and how high you will have to lift your foot and leg in order to cross over the bar. Remember that you are only thinking these things, you are not moving. Now, once you have decided these things, I want you to lift your eyes so that you may no longer see the bar, begin walking forward, cross over the bar, and return to the end of the line.

I shall be directly in front of you when you attempt to cross the bar and shall not let you fall. *Ready:*

Teacher
Instruction: All objectives should be stressed in Part 1 and Part 2. Special emphasis should be placed on estimation and judgment in Part 2.

After each student takes his turn with the bar on the lowest rung, the bar should be gradually raised, one rung at a time, to the maximum height over which the children are capable of stepping. Each child should have his turn at the different heights.

Extreme structure and no talking.

3. THINK AND CHOOSE

Equipment: Squares and rectangles laid out on the floor in varying sizes and constructed from colored tape according to Chapter 6, Diagram 14.

Objective: Body awareness, body position, space awareness, body in space, judgment, coordination.

*Student
Instruction:*   I want half of the group to line up on this side of the room (indicate which half), and the remaining half to line up on this side of the room. The two groups will face each other and there should be at least three feet between each of you. (Indicate amount of space.)

Now I want each of you to stand very still and think of an activity you would like to perform. Next, decide on a square or a rectangle in which you think you can perform your activity. You may want to do a forward roll, or hop on one foot, or rock on your stomach, or any number of things. But remember, you must be able to perform your activity inside the square or rectangle; you must not let your bodies get outside the lines. *Ready:*

*Teacher
Instruction:*   Emphasize body position and body movement in a given amount of space. This activity may be performed by all of the students at once providing there is extreme structure and no talking. The smaller and younger children will need help and encouragement as they will have little conception as to what their bodies can do in a given amount of space.

Mountain Climb

4. MOUNTAIN CLIMB

Equipment: Two inclined planes pushed together and securely fastened to form the "mountain." See Chapter 6, Diagram 15.

Objective: Body awareness on different planes, body position in space, body control, balance.

Student
Instruction: Each of you will line up, one behind the other, at this end of the mountain. One at a time you will cross the mountain. At first you will be climbing and going up; then you will be going down the mountain.

As you climb, and as you go down, let your bodies help you keep your balance. You may need to bend a little forward as you climb up and you may need to lean a little backward as you go down.

The first time you attempt your climb you may watch your feet if necessary; the second time you take your turn, I shall want you to keep your eyes on the target on the wall in front of you; and the third time you will climb the mountain with a bean bag on your head, keeping your eyes once again on the target in front of you. *Ready:*

*Teacher
Instruction:*   All objectives should be stressed throughout the activity. Stress bending the body as little as possible.

For the very young child it may be necessary to hold his hand on the first few attempts. Emphasize also the different plane on which the child will be walking and "feeling" his way rather than watching his feet.

Extreme structure and no talking.

5. POSITIONS IN SPACE

Equipment: Space enough for each child to lie on the floor with all limbs extended, leaving at least four feet between each child when in this position.

Objective: Body awareness on different planes, body position in space, body control, balance, body image, coordination, directionality.

*Student
Instruction:*   Each of you find a space on the floor, lie down on your back, extend all of your limbs, like this, and then be sure there is still this much room between yourself and any other student around you. (Indicate amount of space.)

Part 1.   Lie on your back, feet together and hands by your side. First raise your head off the floor, then your shoulders. Next, raise your left arm and then your right arm. Now, holding this position, raise your left leg and then your right leg and finally the lower part of your back until nearly all of your body is in space; and yet you are still in contact with the floor.

Part 2.   Turn on your stomach with your feet together, hands by your sides, and your face toward the floor. First raise your face and head off the floor, then your shoulders. Next raise your left arm and then your right arm. Now, holding this position, raise your left leg and then your right leg and finally your chest until nearly all of your body is in space; and yet, you are still in contact with the floor.

Part 3. Turn on your left side with your feet together, one leg on top of the other; arms above your head, resting on the floor, one arm on top of the other with your head resting between your arms. (Demonstrate position.)

First raise your arms and your head off the floor as high as you are able. Next, begin to raise your shoulders and your chest. You will feel a pull on your side as you next begin to raise your waist off the floor. Holding this position, slowly raise your feet and legs off the floor as high as you are able. Now, think about where your body is: nearly all in space and yet you are still in contact with the floor.

Part 4. Repeat instructions as in Part 3 lying on right side of body.

Teacher Instruction: Stress all objectives with an emphasis on the gradual lifting of the body into space.

Part 3 and Part 4 will be difficult for the child and should be demonstrated on the first few attempts.

6. GROWING TREES

Equipment: Space enough for each child to lie on the floor with all limbs extended, leaving at least four feet between each child when in this position. Two beanbags for each child.

Objective: Body and space awareness, body position in space, body image, body control, balance, coordination, abstraction.

Student Instruction: Each of you find a space on the floor, lie down on your back, extend all of your limbs, like this, and then be sure there is still this much room between yourself and any other student around you. (Indicate amount of space.)

Part 1.   First we are going to pretend that we are all trees lying down upon the ground. Make your bodies straight, put your legs and feet together, and move your arms out to the side so they are in line with your shoulders, like this. Now, turn your hands so your palms are downward, like this.

I shall walk around to each of you and on each of your hands I am going to place a beanbag. Who can tell me what the beanbags are going to be? (The answer should be that the beanbags are bird nests; give clues until you get this answer.) Yes, they are bird nests. I want you to listen first to my instructions, lying very still. We are going to pretend that you, the tree, are going to grow back, straight and tall. But you have two bird nests on your limbs and you must not drop them while you are growing. Your feet are your roots and when you have finished growing, you will be standing on your roots, straight and tall, with your limbs out to the side, each holding a bird nest.

When you begin to grow, you will first raise your head off the floor, then your shoulders and your arms. Next raise your back and waist until you are in a sitting position. Pull your feet up, let your body lean a little forward and raise yourself up into a standing position. You must never bend your elbows and your arms must be kept straight out to the sides of your body at all times. *Ready:*

Part 2.   Once again you are going to pretend that you are a tree which has fallen to the ground. You will begin growing again until you are straight and tall. This time, however, the bird nest is right on your forehead. Begin by raising your head just as you did before; only this time you must drop your head backward and keep it in this position, so as not to drop the bird nest. *Ready:*

Part 3.   (Repeat Part 1, giving same instructions, adding the fact that the eyes must be kept closed at all times.)

Teacher
Instruction: All objectives should be stressed with an emphasis placed on control of the body parts holding the bean bags.

Each part should be attempted several times and the children will encounter difficulty in performing the activity when the eyes are closed. In the case of very young children or children with an extreme motor deficit, you may want to have them raise only to a sitting position during the first attempts.

Extreme structure and no talking.

7. ROPE THROW

Equipment: Two lengths of rope 15 ft. in length with enough weight to form different patterns on the floor when thrown up into the air.

Objective: Eye-foot coordination, body control, body coordination, balance, visual-tactual proficiency, body movement through space.

*Student
Instruction:* I am going to divide you into two groups. This group will line up, one behind the other, behind this pile of rope with at least three feet of space between each of you. (Indicate rope placement and amount of space between each child.) The other group will line up in the same way behind this pile of rope.

Part 1. When I say *Ready,* the first person in each line will pick up the pile of rope and throw it out and away from him into the air. When it falls to the floor, it will make a pattern on the floor.

Look at the pattern it has made very carefully before beginning; then step on one of the ends of the rope and, heel-to-toe fashion, walk your way to the other end. Use your eyes as well as your feet in telling you where to go. *Ready:*

Part 2. (Repeat Part 1 with eyes closed eliminating visual reinforcement and stressing the tactual aspect.)

*Teacher
Instruction:* All objectives should be stressed in this activity. Emphasize the tactual aspect in placing the foot squarely on top of the rope in order to maintain balance.

For very young and small children, it may be necessary to first practice throwing the rope.

Extreme structure and no talking.

8. MECHANICAL IMITATIONS

Equipment: Space enough for each child to lie down on the floor with all limbs extended, having at least four feet between himself and any other child around him when in this position.

Objective: Body and body parts awareness, body image, body in space, body in motion, abstraction.

Student
Instruction: I want all of you to find space upon the floor, lie down, and extend all of your limbs like this. You will need at least this much space between yourself and any other student. (Indicate amount of space.) If there isn't this much space, then I shall help you find another space on the floor.

Now that we have our positions, put your feet together, your arms and hands by your sides, and listen carefully.

You are going to be doing imitations, with your bodies, of things that move. I shall call out a name of something; for example, an airplane, or a tractor, or perhaps a spinning top. When I call out the name of the object, you will continue to lie still and simply think. Think about how different parts of your body might imitate, or take the place of, the moving parts of the object I have named. Then when I say *go,* you may begin your imitations.

While you are doing your imitation, you may take any position you like as long as you do not take up any more space than that which has been demonstrated to you. You may stand, sit, lie down on your back, on your stomach, or place your body in any position you want to in order to do your imitation.

Try to have as many different parts of your body in motion at the same time as is possible, but only your body in action, not your voice. Do *not* imitate the motor of the airplane, for example, through the use of your voice.

You will all be doing your imitations at the same time, but when you hear me say *Stop,* you will all return to your lying-down positions on the floor to wait for me to call the next object or thing you will imitate. *Ready:*

1. Airplane
2. Car
3. Hook and Ladder Fire Engine
4. Egg Beater
5. Horse on a Carrousel
6. Ditch-Digger
7. Helicopter
8. Spinning Top
9. Tree in a Strong Wind
10. Tornado
11. Smoke Rising out of a Chimney
12. Rocking Horse
13. Waves on the Ocean

Teacher Instruction:

Stress all objectives emphasizing having as many different parts of the body in motion at the same time as is possible.

In this activity spacing of the children on the floor is important and you will need to help them find an appropriate amount of space.

This activity may be extremely stimulating. There must, therefore, be extreme structure and no talking.

9. JUMPING ROPE

Equipment: Lengths of jumping rope for each child in the class.

Objective: Body and body parts awareness, body image, body in space, rhythm, general coordination, eye-foot coordination, spatial relationships, visual direction of movement.

Student Instruction:

I am going to divide the class into two groups: Group 1 and Group 2. (Divide class and indicate which is Group 1 and which is Group 2.) I want Group 1 to be seated at this end of the room. Group 2 will form a line, with each of you side by side, facing me, and with at least three feet of space between each of you. (Indicate amount of space and where line is to be formed.)

First I shall hand each of you in Group 2 a jumping rope which you will simply hold until I have told you what to do.

Now that you are in position with your ropes, I want you to lay your rope down in front of you; lay it straight; and lay it about this far in front of your feet. (Demonstrate.) Reach down and pick up both ends with each of your hands, leaving the middle of the rope touching the floor. Now, with your feet together, jump over the rope. This now places the rope behind you.

The next thing I want you to do is to begin moving your arms, back, up, over your head, down, and to your sides. You are now in the same position from which you started, with the rope lying in front of your feet.

This is what we are going to do, over and over, getting faster and faster, until it is just one motion and until we are jumping rope. We shall begin very slowly. *Ready:*

Teacher
Instruction: Stress the individual steps necessary in rope jumping with an emphasis on visually determining when the rope will be in position for jumping.

In the beginning stages this is a difficult activity for nearly all children. The most common problem is over-anticipation and jumping too soon. Stress here that the rope must actually be hitting the floor when the jump is made.

The time allowed for each group to actively participate will be determined by the ability of the children as well as the amount of time allowed for the program.

10. TRAMPOLINE

Equipment: Trampoline, preferably a 5 X 10 size bed.

Objective: Body and body parts awareness, body image, body in space, body control, general coordination, balance, rhythm, response to verbal command, direction of body movement.

Student
Instruction: I want all of you to form a line, side by side, here in front of the trampoline, with at least three feet of space between each of you. (Indicate amount of space.) Be seated exactly where you are and listen carefully.

We are going to be jumping on the trampoline, one at a time. At no time will there be more than one person on the trampoline unless it is when I am working with one of you. When it is your turn, however, and you are jumping, there will be three other students working in the activity. These three other students will be Spotters and will take their places, one at each end, and one on the side across from where I shall be. (Indicate these four positions.)

The Spotters' job is a very important one, and that is to keep the jumper from ever falling off the trampoline. If a jumper gets too close to your edge, you raise your arms and hands and push the jumper back toward the center of the bed. This may cause the jumper to fall on the bed, but it will not hurt him.

The Spotter will need to do this only if a student fails to follow the instructions I give. So this is one job I don't ever want you to have to perform.

Part 1. I want the first student in line to crawl onto the trampoline here beside me. When you get on the trampoline, always get on beside me; and when you get off, always get off beside me. This is true even for those of you who may have been jumping for several years. When you climb onto the trampoline, never step on the springs. Place your weight on the frame, and then right on over onto the bed. (Indicate the springs, the frame, and the bed.)

Now that you are on the trampoline, I want you to crawl over to the red *X* in the middle and sit on the *X.* I shall begin bouncing the trampoline with my hands and I want you to let your body rise and fall, remaining in a sitting position as much as possible. Use your hands if you feel yourself falling to one side or the other. Keep your back and head straight and your eyes looking straight forward.

(After no longer than two minutes): Now, crawl back over to where I am, get off the trampoline and return to the end of the line. Remember, do not step on or place your hands on the springs. Place your weight on the frame and then off and onto the floor.

We shall do many activities on the trampoline and this is the first. After each of you has had his turn, we shall go on to the next. Beginning with the second activity, I shall demonstrate the activitity before the first student takes his turn. *Ready:*

Part 2. (Little Bounce) Stand on the X and begin to bounce your body without lifting your feet off the bed.

Part 3. (Big Bounce) Stand on the X and begin to bounce your body, lifting your feet off the bed each time you bounce.

Part 4. (Seat Drop) Begin with two big bounces, lean the body slightly back, and begin to bend the body at the hips into a sitting position.

At the same time, the arms are drawn back and behind the seat, with the hands palms down toward the bed, and fingers pointing toward the seat. The legs are thrown forward, straight and with toes pointed. The landing should be flat with the seat, hands, legs and heels all landing at once.

Part 5. (Knee Drop) Begin with two big bounces. When the body lifts as if beginning a third bounce, the feet are drawn up and behind resulting in a drop to the knees.

As the drop to the knees begins, the arms are drawn behind the body, swung through when the knees are on the bed, and then forward and up.

The back should be kept straight at all times during the activity and the height of the bouncing should be kept to a minimum.

Teacher
Instruction: All objectives should be stressed with an emphasis on keeping the body erect, with control and propulsion of the body through the arm movements.

It is imperative that the safety factor be stressed and that spotters be used. It is doubtful that the spotters will ever have occasion to push a child back toward the center, but they should be prepared. You should always stop the activity a child is performing the instant he begins to move away from the X denoting the center of the bed.

This is one of the most valuable activities for all children, especially for children with learning disabilities who manifest a deficit in the areas of general body coordination, space concept, and body control. Trampolining does not have to be dangerous; it is not unless directions are purposely disobeyed.

For the very young child and for those with a fear of the trampoline, you should be on the bed performing each activity with the child in the beginning stages. It might also be wise to surround the trampoline with pads in order to facilitate mounting and dismounting.

All activities should be performed in stocking feet and under no circumstances should the "play-type" trampoline be used.

Regardless of ability, no one child should be allowed on the trampoline for more than two minutes at a time.

Extreme structure and no talking. All commands given in a rhythmic manner.

10. SPACE TRAVEL

Equipment: Area large enough for children to form two teams and with at least thirty feet in front of them in which to perform their activity.

Objective: Body movement through space, laterality, directionality, balance, body control, body awareness, body position, general coordination.

*Student
Instruction:*

Listen carefully as I call the names of half of the class. As I call your name, I want you to line up, one behind the other, in front of me at this end of the room.

Now I want all of you who are left to line up, one behind the other, in front of me and next to the first team.

I am going to move to the other end of the room and from that position I will tell each of you, in pairs, how you are to move your bodies through space from where you are to where I am. I will not tell you exactly how to move but I will give you hints as to how you are to move.

The two of you who are first in line on each team will start together after I have given you your instructions and when I say, "Begin." After you reach me, you will turn, walk back to your team and take your place at the end of the line. Each of you will then take your turn in the same manner.

Remember, this is not a race. What counts is the way you move your bodies through space. *Ready:*

(The following directions are given, a different direction being given to each pair of children.)

1. Move through space with your body facing forward.
2. Move through space with your left side forward.
3. Move through space with your right side forward.
4. Move through space with your back toward me.
5. Move through space with your hands touching the floor.
6. Move through space with your body touching the floor.
7. Move through space with only one foot touching the floor.
8. Move through space with your body bent low.
9. Move through space with your body tall and straight.
10. Move through space very fast.
11. Move through space very slowly.
12. Move through space any way you like.

*Teacher
Instruction:*

Although this activity appears quite simple, it is usually most difficult for children with perceptual deficits. As the activity is repeated, however, the children become more capable of deciding upon and initiating their own activities according to the instruction.

It is important that enough time be allowed for each child in the pair to perform as well as he is able. For this reason, it should be continually stressed that this is not a racing type activity and that the members of the class must not be urging the active participants to hurry. This only causes pressure on the child attempting to carry out the activity.

An awareness of movement through space should be emphasized as well as the different positions of the body while movement is occurring.

Extreme structure and no talking should be encouraged although this is a somewhat stimulating activity.

12. MY SHADOW

Equipment: Area large enough for children to form two lines with each child facing the instructor and with at least four feet between each child when arms are outstretched.

Objective: Body and space awareness, body position, body control, coordination, reproduction of specific body movements, laterality, directionality, visual and auditory motor matching.

Student Instruction: I want this half of the group (indicate which half) to form a line which will reach from this side of the room to that side of the room and with each of you facing me. Stretch your arms out to the sides of your body and then move apart from one another until there is this much room between each of you (indicate amount of room).

(The same instruction is then given to the remaining half of the class, having them form their line in front of the first group.)

Listen carefully. I am going to stand in front of you with my back to you. This is so we all will be facing the same direction.

You are going to be my shadows. This means that after I
say and do something, you will say and do just exactly the
same thing. I will be saying the activity as I am doing the
activity. So, you will need to look and listen at the same
time. You will begin saying and doing your activity just as
soon as I finish saying and doing my activity. When you
complete your activity, hold your final position until I say
and begin a new activity.

We will say and do our activities in groups of four, then
we will pause for a moment. We will say and do four more
activities, pause, and so on. *Ready:*

1. I am bending forward
    (Children repeat and perform activity.)
    I have stretched my arms way out
    (Children repeat and perform activity.)
    I am bending backward
    (Children repeat and perform activity.)
    Now I'm turning round and about.
    (Children repeat and perform activity.)

(The above procedure is carried out on each of the following.)

2. I am bending to the left
    I am turning around
    I am bending to the right
    Now I'm standing without a sound.

3. I am jumping up and down
    I have rolled into a ball
    I am crawling on the floor
    Now I've grown up very tall.

4. I am rolling my head around
    I am shaking the top of me
    I am standing on one foot
    Now I'm kneeling on one knee.

5. I am standing flat on my feet
    I am standing on my heels
    I have brought my feet together
    Now my body reels and reels.

6. I am standing on my tip toes
    I am stretched on the floor
       like a rubber band

I am sitting down on both my heels
Now I'm waving my left hand.

7. I am standing with my legs quite bent
    I am standing with my legs apart
    I am standing up on one leg only
    Now I'm standing straight as a dart.

Teaching
Instruction: Emphasis should be placed on the many and varied body positions, precise execution of command and rhythm. The amount of body movement in a given amount of space also should be stressed.

Repeated practice will be required before this activity is performed with accuracy to the point that objectives are being met. With very small children, it probably will be necessary to demonstrate each of the positions before entering into the full activity.

The rhyming effect of each group of four activities should eventually be noted by the children and should serve as auditory reinforcement.

As the children become more experienced, they should be allowed to say and do the activities with the instructor rather than following the instructor.

Extreme structure and no talking.

Related Reading References

Chaney, Clara M. and Newell C. Kephart. *Motoric Aids to Perceptual Training.* Columbus, Ohio: Charles E. Merrill Publishing Co., 1968, pp. 88-91, 93-111. A presentation of the basic motor and perceptual activities for training children with learning disorders, including the brain injured and retarded.

Cratty, Bryant J. and Sister Margaret Mary Martin, *Perceptual-Motor Efficiency in Children.* Philadelphia: Lea and Febiger, 1969, pp. 49, 156-163. A program for the development of perceptual-motor efficiency based on principles of child development with an emphasis on the importance of motivating children to learn and the use of movement activities as an aid to learning.

Kephart, Newell C. *The Slow Learner in the Classroom.* 2nd ed. Columbus, Ohio: Charles E. Merrill Publishing Co., 1971, pp. 79-104, 143-168, 218-224. A systematic approach to the identification of slow learner behavior and learning problems including techniques for identifying and correcting specific disabilities.

Teaching through Sensory-Motor Experiences. John I. Arena, ed. San Rafael, California: Academic Therapy Publications, 1969, pp. 47-62, 77-85. A compilation of articles in which the authors, all experienced in working with children, focus on those areas that they have found to be poorly developed or inefficiently and inconsistently integrated in functionally underachieving children. Emphasis is placed on a series of more basic skills which must first develop and become integrated before communication skills are established.

Valett, Robert E. *Programming Learning Disabilities.* Palo Alto, California: Fearon Publishers, 1969, pp. 15-20, 117-118, 159-162. A practical framework for the actual programming of learning disabilities with an attempt at bridging the gap between existing theory and practice. Covered are the three stages in programming consisting of planning, implementation and remediation.

_____ "The Remediation of Learning Disabilities" (Tabbed Section on *Gross Motor Development #11*), Palo Alto, California: Fearon Publishers, 1967. A comprehensive and specific program including resource material for children with specific learning disabilities. Six major areas of learning are covered: Gross Motor Development, Sensory-Motor Integration, Perceptual-Motor Skills, Language Development, Conceptual Skills, and Social Skills.

chapter 6

TEACHING GUIDELINES FOR
POTENTIAL THROUGH PERCEPTION

1. Be clear and concise in giving all instructions.
2. Give instruction only with the individual attention of each child.
3. Give all commands in a rhythmic tone of voice.
4. Give instruction in a logical sequential order.
5. Keep all terminology on a level geared to the child's understanding.
6. Be prepared to give instructions over and over again if necessary.
7. Keep your voice calm; outbursts indicate disapproval and rejection.
8. Space the children in order to avoid any temptation to bother a neighbor.
9. Remove all outside stimulation.
10. Be sure every child is working in his stocking feet; even tennis shoes may cause stumbling and tripping.
11. Encourage each child to attempt every activity.
12. Be certain the child is not becoming overly tired.
13. Constructively criticize, not allowing a child to repeatedly perform an activity incorrectly.
14. Let the child progress as rapidly as possible.
15. Give the child as much time as is necessary and practical in performing an activity.
16. Evaluate daily the progress of each child.
17. Adjust to progress coming slowly.
18. Offer praise and acceptance on every possible occasion.
19. Stress safety throughout the entire program.
20. *Expect* more than is evident in each child's performance; but *be prepared* to *accept* less.

Implementation of Program

PHYSICAL REQUIREMENTS

PERSONNEL

Potential through Perception was designed and developed with such structure and explicit instruction so as to enable a single classroom teacher to carry out the program on a daily basis in a public school setting. The program met with success in a situation such as this in the initial research program in the Lubbock Public Schools, Lubbock, Texas.

The program in its entirety, now being carried out at Heritage Hall, Private School for Children with Learning Disabilities in Lubbock, employs a somewhat different procedure.

Four instructors are involved in working with each class, with each instructor having his or her station within the Perceptual Training Room and working specifically in one of the four perceptual training areas: Perceptual Motor, Ocular Motor, Auditory Motor, and Body and Space Awareness.

The class is divided into four groups with the groups rotating from one station to the next for instruction. This procedure enables each child, during the daily one hour Perceptual Training period, to have instruction in each of the perceptual areas.

PLANT

A room which could be permanently facilitated for Perceptual Training would be the ideal situation. If this is not possible, then the teaching classroom may adequately be used. Student desks will need to be moved against the walls and the necessary perceptual equipment brought out daily. With, however, structure and cooperation on the part of the children, the time element involved here is minimal.

LENGTH OF PERIOD

The length of the daily Perceptual Training period will depend primarily upon three factors:

> 1. Age of the children
> 2. Achievement level of the children
> 3. Size of the class

If as many as twelve children are receiving instruction in a single class period, an hour each day should be allowed. Under no circumstances should less than forty-five minutes be allowed. A session involving less than forty-five minutes does not adequately allow for instruction, correction, and evaluation as well.

LENGTH OF PROGRAM

Potential through perception can well be expected to cover an entire school year. For a group of very young children and for groups where extreme deficits persist, it is doubtful that more than half of the program can be adequately covered during the year.

In every instance, a new program in Perceptual Training should involve all four areas of instruction as progress in one area will speed progress in each of the other areas. The child will not receive full benefit if, for example, the Perceptual Motor Activities are completed before Ocular Motor Activities are begun; or if Ocular Motor Activities are completed before Auditory Motor Activities are begun.

Here again, we must determine the length of an activity or the length of an entire program on the basis of the needs of the individual child. At all times, do as much as is possible, for as many as is possible, with what we have at hand.

EQUIPMENT AND MATERIALS SPECIFICATIONS

Equipment necessary for the Perceptual Training program does not necessarily need to be expensive. Specifications for building and constructing most of the equipment can be found in the following pages.

Items such as balls, Indian clubs, etc. will have to be purchased, but the cost should be nominal.

The school should be able to provide a piano for this period during the day, leaving only the trampoline as a major expense.

DIAGRAM 1

RHYTHM STEPS (Perceptual Motor Activity #4)

Two-by-two inch crosses constructed of one-half inch colored tape, placed on the floor according to diagram below.

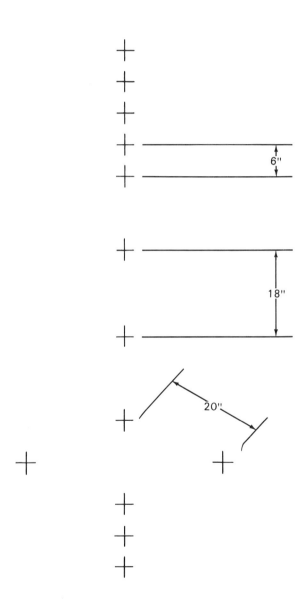

DIAGRAM 2

ROCKING BOARD (Perceptual Motor Activity #5)

Rocking board constructed of ¾ inch plyboard according to diagram below.

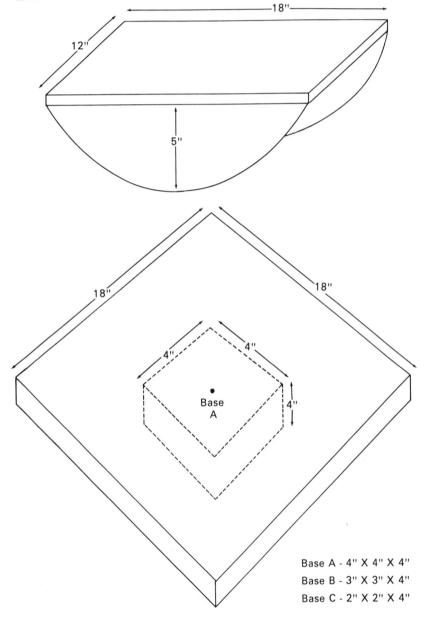

Base A - 4" X 4" X 4"
Base B - 3" X 3" X 4"
Base C - 2" X 2" X 4"

DIAGRAM 3   *(Facing page)*

BALANCE BOARD (Perceptual Motor Activity #6)

Balance board constructed of ¾ inch plyboard according to diagram above. Bases attached to board, with ⅜" bolt with wing nut. Bases are changed according to the degree of difficulty desired. The smaller the base, the more difficult the activity becomes.

DIAGRAM 4

STAIR STEPS (Perceptual Motor Activity #7)

MUSICAL STAIRS (Auditory Motor Activity #6)

Stairs constructed of ¾ inch plyboard according to diagram below.

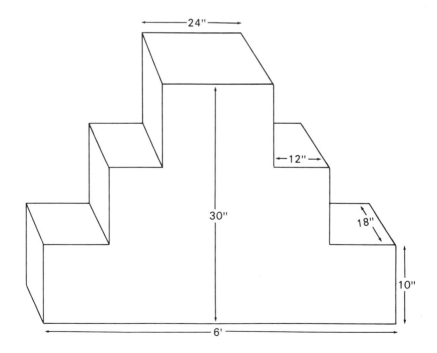

DIAGRAM 5

COLOR MAZE (Auditory Motor Activity #1)

Twenty-eight five-by-five inch squares cut from red, yellow, blue and green oilcloth, seven of each color, placed on the floor according to the diagram below. The spacing will vary according to the size of the children.

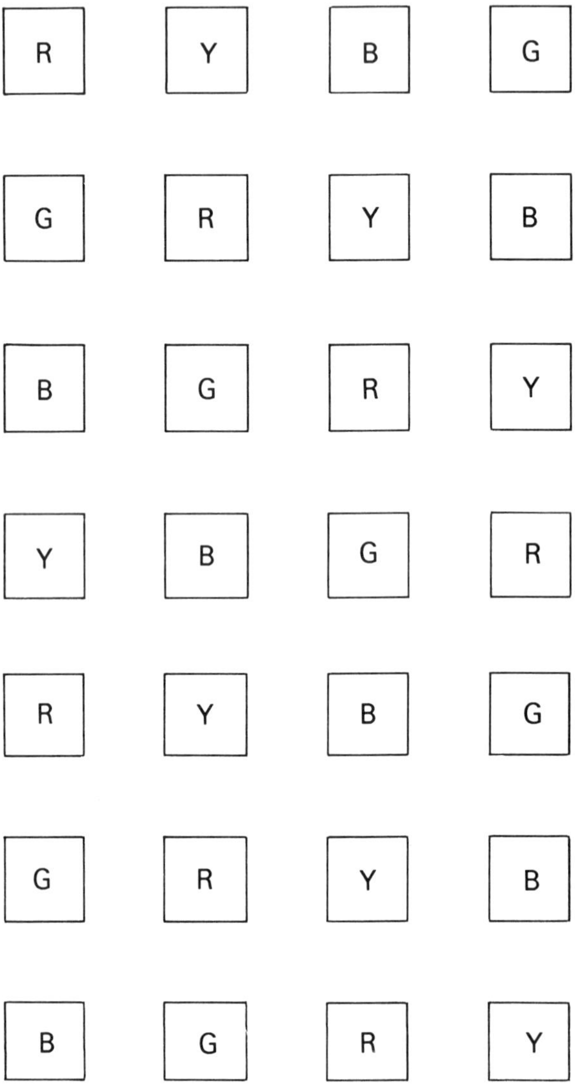

R	Y	B	G
G	R	Y	B
B	G	R	Y
Y	B	G	R
R	Y	B	G
G	R	Y	B
B	G	R	Y

DIAGRAM 6

OBSTACLE COURSE (Auditory Motor Activity #10)

Two Indian clubs, one three-foot length of rope, one nine-by-nine inch
cardboard square, one nine-inch diameter cardboard circle, one nine-by-
fifteen inch cardboard rectangle, one rocking board arranged according to
diagram below with four feet between each article.

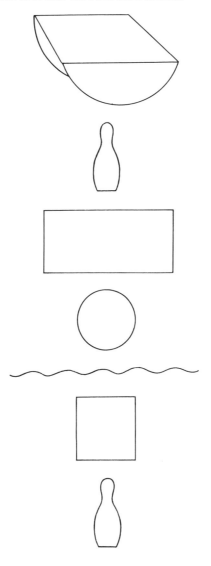

DIAGRAM 7

THE WALKING STUMPS (Ocular Motor Activity #1)

Ten blocks of wood, each with a 12" surface top, varying in height from 6" to 18"; 3 *A*'s, 2 *B*'s, 2 *C*'s, and 3 *D*'s placed on the floor according to the diagram below.

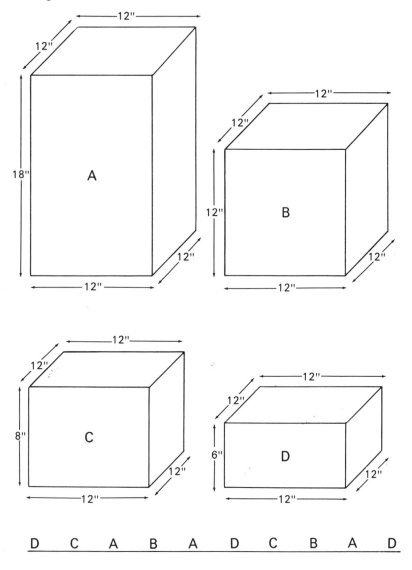

D   C   A   B   A   D   C   B   A   D

DIAGRAM 8

SWINGING BALL (Ocular Motor Activity #3)
(Ocular Motor Activity #4)

Swinging ball attached to the ceiling according to diagram below. Flash-cards constructed of 5" X 5" cardboard numbered from 1–10 with size of numbers varying from 1" to 3".

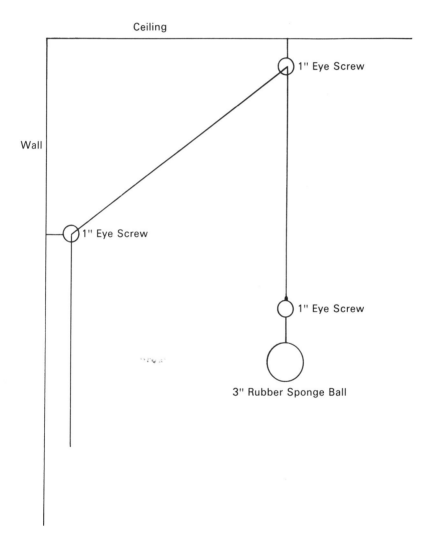

DIAGRAM 9

READY, AIM, FIRE (Ocular Motor Activity #5)

A 3 ft. by 3 ft. pegboard constructed according to diagram below with ¼ inch area surrounding each hole painted according to indicated colors: B (Blue), G (Green), Y (Yellow), R (Red). Pegs sufficient in number for children in class.

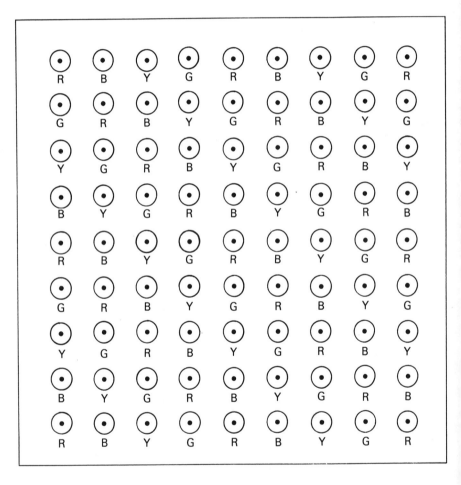

DIAGRAM 10

VISUAL TRACKING AND STEERING CHARTS (Ocular Motor Activity #7)

Charts constructed on 22" X 28" cardboard according to diagram below; patterns to be found on the following 2 pages.

Chart 1

Chart 2

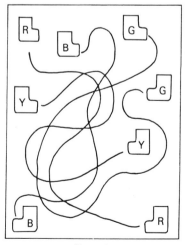

Chart 3

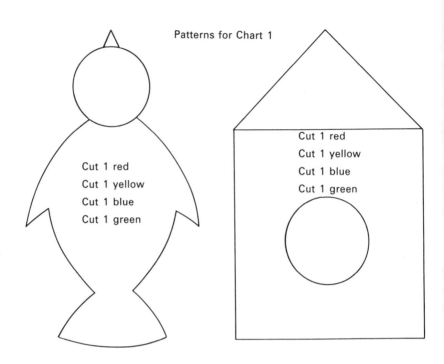

Patterns for Chart 1

Cut 1 red
Cut 1 yellow
Cut 1 blue
Cut 1 green

Cut 1 red
Cut 1 yellow
Cut 1 blue
Cut 1 green

Patterns for Chart 3

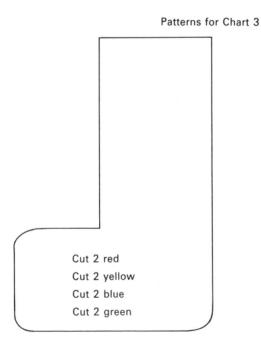

Cut 2 red
Cut 2 yellow
Cut 2 blue
Cut 2 green

Patterns for Chart 2

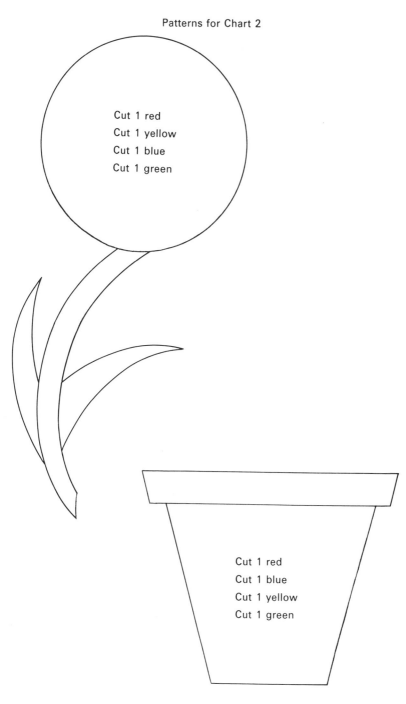

Cut 1 red
Cut 1 yellow
Cut 1 blue
Cut 1 green

Cut 1 red
Cut 1 blue
Cut 1 yellow
Cut 1 green

DIAGRAM 11

NUMBER MAZE (Ocular Motor Activity #9)

Twenty-eight five-by-five inch squares cut from yellow oilcloth, each with
a number printed on the square arranged according to diagram below.

24	1	23	22
20	19	3	21
18	17	16	2
14	13	1	15
12	11	3	10
7	2	8	9
1	4	5	6

DIAGRAM 12

WALKING PATHS AND WALKING BOARD (Ocular Motor Activity #10)

Walking board and paths of green oilcloth constructed according to diagram below. Wand constructed of ¼ in. dowel with 1½ in. rubber ball attached to end.

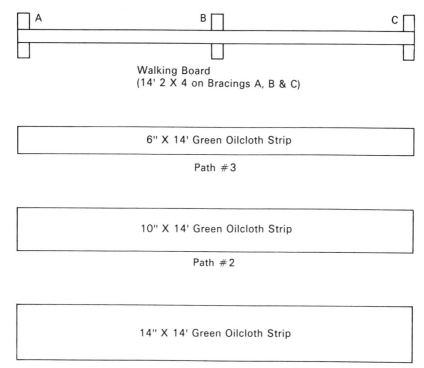

Walking Board
(14' 2 X 4 on Bracings A, B & C)

6" X 14' Green Oilcloth Strip

Path #3

10" X 14' Green Oilcloth Strip

Path #2

14" X 14' Green Oilcloth Strip

Path #1

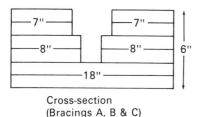

Cross-section
(Bracings A, B & C)

Bracings constructed of 2 X 4's
cut to specified lengths and
nailed together according to
diagram

DIAGRAM 13

OVER AND UNDER SPACE BAR (Body and Space Awareness Activity #2)

Over-and-under space bar constructed of two 6' 2 X 2's according to diagram below. Dowels to hold bar constructed of ¼" doweling set in 2 X 2's, extending out 1" and spaced 6" apart.

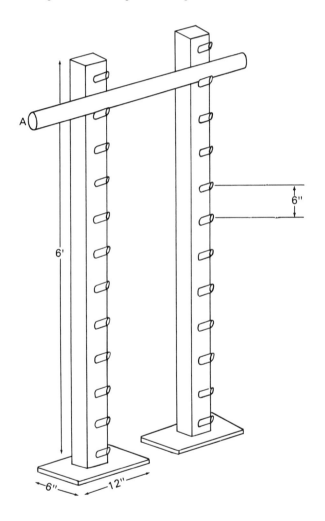

DIAGRAM 14

THINK AND CHOOSE (Body and Space Awareness Activity #3)

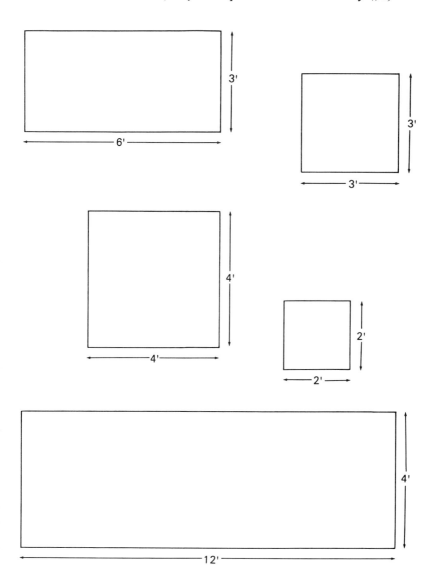

DIAGRAM 15

MOUNTAIN CLIMB (Body and Space Awareness Activity #4)

Two inclined planes constructed of ¾ inch plyboard pushed together and securely fastened according to diagram below.

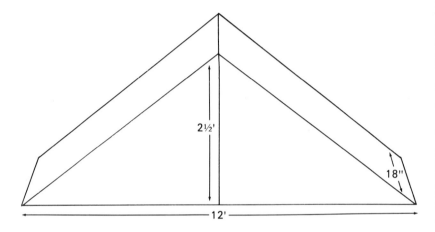

General References

Ashlock, Patrick and Alberta Stephen. *Educational Therapy in the Elementary School.* Springfield, Illinois: Charles C. Thomas, 1966. An attempt to draw together the relevant findings of other disciplines which deal, in whole or in part, with the learning problems of children. A concept which encompasses the findings of these disciplines, while dedicating itself exclusively to the educational problems of the child who has difficulty learning academic material. A summary of the principles, methods and materials which have been used successfully with children who have learning problems.

Benyon, Sheila Doran. *Intensive Programming for Slow Learners.* Columbus, Ohio: Charles E. Merrill Publishing Co., 1963. A presentation of an intensified six-week training program aimed at training student teachers for diagnostic teaching in a classroom and providing an atmosphere for structured learning through the utilization of perceptual-motor techniques. Preparations for the establishment of such a program are presented as well as detailed activities used throughout the six-week program at Purdue University.

Bush, Wilma Jo and Marian Taylor Giles. *Aids to Psycholinguistic Teaching.* Columbus, Ohio: Charles E. Merrill Publishing Co., 1969. A comprehensive explanation of specific psycholinguistic disabilities with a frame of reference for developing diagnostic teaching procedures. Developmental and remedial activities are presented in detail and grouped by interest and difficulty levels from first to eighth grade levels.

Dillon, Edward J., Earl J. Heath, and Carroll W. Biggs. *Comprehensive Programming for Success in Learning.* Columbus, Ohio: Charles E. Merrill Publishing Co., 1970. A study covering the first two years of the three-year *Project Child* in which emphasis is placed upon an educationally relevant school system for children in the rapidly changing urban areas. Coordination of efforts including early identification of problem learners, continuous in-service training of teachers, interdisciplinary teams at the guiding level, and information dissemination is thoroughly presented.

Ebersole, Marylou, Newell C. Kephart, and James B. Ebersole, *Steps to Achievement for the Slow Learner.* Columbus, Ohio: Charles E. Merrill Publishing Co., 1968. A systematic approach to the understanding of early childhood training for the child with brain dysfunction including both theory and curriculum.

Farrald, Robert R., Frances Hargis, and Vinson M. Jester. *A Remediation Handbook for Children with Reading Disabilities.* Edinburg, Texas: Region One Education Service Center. The objective of this "Remediation Handbook for Children with Reading Disabilities" is to help the classroom teacher to diagnose and remediate the various kinds of problems grouped under the heading of "reading disability."

Frierson, Edward C. and Walter B. Barbe. *Educating Children with Learning Disabilities: Selected Readings.* New York: Appleton-Century-Crofts, 1967. Selections providing a systematic introduction and guide to a more intensive study of special learning disabilities in children. Appeal should be to the general educator as well as to the clinical specialist or college instructor.

Getman, G. N., and E. R. Kane. *The Physiology of Readiness ... An Action Program for the Development of Perception for Children.* Minneapolis: Programs to Accelerate School Success, 1964. A readiness program based on a pilot experimental program conducted during 1963 in the first grade classrooms of the Golden Valley School District (a Minneapolis, Minnesota, suburb). Hypothesis: Readiness for academic tasks can be systematically developed on a physiological basis and such higher levels of readiness contribute directly and significantly to childrens' academic success. (In this case, reading performance.)

Haeussermann, Else. *Developmental Potential of Preschool Children: an Evaluation of Intellectual, Sensory and Emotional Functioning.* New York: Grune and Stratton, 1958. A textbook for the clinical evaluation of behavioral functions in the brain-damaged or retarded child.

Johnson, Doris J. and Helmer R. Myklebust. *Learning Disabilities—Educational Principles and Practices.* New York: Grune and Stratton, 1967. A textbook with an approach to remediation aimed at training teachers, as well as other educators and specialists concerned with learning disabilities. The volume presents a frame of reference, principles and practices, emphasizing the psychoneurological aspect.

Kaluger, George, and Clifford J. Kolson. *Reading and Learning Disabilities.* Columbus, Ohio: Charles E. Merrill Publishing Co., 1969. Applicable for the reading teacher, classroom and specialist, interested in remedial work and for the psychologist or other specialist in diagnosing learning problems. Tools for pinpointing individual reading problems are presented as well as specific guidelines for tailoring a remedial program to an individual's particular learning problem.

Kephart, Newell C. *The Slow Learner in the Classroom.* 2nd. ed. Columbus, Ohio: Charles E. Merrill Publishing Co., 1971. A systematic approach to the identification of slow learner behavior and learning problems including techniques for identifying and correcting specific disabilities.

McCarthy, James J., and Joan F. McCarthy. *Learning Disabilities.* Boston: Allyn and Bacon, 1969. A review of the theories and status of learning disabilities. A presentation of the consensus and viewpoints of diverse authors, a synthesization of the divergent points of view, and a description of the major remedial methods advocated.

Myers, Patricia I. and Donald D. Hammill, *Methods for Learning Disorders.* New York: John Wiley & Sons, 1969. A theoretical frame of reference within which to view the learning disorders of children, to provide methods of teaching learning disabled children, to provide an overview of learning disorders for use by professional personnel, and to suggest a descriptive orientation for assessment and remediation of learning disorders.

Peter, Laurence J. *Prescriptive Teaching.* New York: McGraw-Hill, 1965. A textbook dealing with the means of achieving sound educational goals for disturbed or handicapped children based on an interdisciplinary approach which accomplishes therapeutic aims by educational means. Methodology for dealing with problems in the regular classroom or in special education is presented.

Radler, D. H. and Newell C. Kephart. *Success Through Play.* New York: Harper & Row, Publishers, 1960. A presentation of simple techniques for helping the pre-school child prepare for school in the development of basic learning and perceptual skills.

Roach, E. G. and Newell C. Kephart. *The Purdue Perceptual-Motor Survey.* Columbus, Ohio: Charles E. Merrill Publishing Co., 1966. A survey to be used as a guide in the observance of many and varied kinds of behavior in a structured framework. The three major areas of concern are laterality, directionality, and the skills of perceptual-motor matching.

Simpson, Dorothy M., *Learning to Learn.* Columbus, Ohio: Charles E. Merrill Publishing Co., 1968. A theoretical approach acquainting the classroom teacher and the parent with processes involved in learning to learn.

Waugh, Kenneth W., and Wilma Jo Bush. *Diagnosing Learning Disorders.* Columbus, Ohio: Charles E. Merrill Publishing Co., 1971. A detailed description of twelve of the most common learning disorders with diagnostic procedures for identification of these behaviors and remediation techniques for specific problem areas. Case studies at the elementary, junior high and senior high school levels are provided.

Winter Haven Lions Research Foundation, Inc. *Procedure Manual—Perceptual Form Training.* Winter Haven, Florida: Star Press, 1963. A home-training program designed as part of a total perceptual procedure that can be employed as a means to assist young children to develop more effective eye-hand-motor skills.

Glossary

Auditory: Of or pertaining to hearing or the sense or organs of hearing.

Conceptualize: To grasp a mental image of a thing formed by generalization from particulars; to have an idea of what a thing in general should be.

Directionality: Of direction in space.

Distractibility: A distracting, or state of being distracted; perplexity; confusion; disorder.

Emotional lability: Unstable. Readily undergoing change. A departure from the normal calm state of an organism of such nature as to include strong feeling, an impulse toward open action, and certain internal physical reactions; any one of the states designated as fear, anger, disgust, grief, joy, surprise, yearning, etc.

Hyperactivity: Abnormal excess in extent or degree of activity.

Hypoactivity: Abnormal decrease, deficiency, or weakness in activity.

Impulsiveness: Acting momentarily, or by impulse.

Kinesthetic: The sense whose end organs lie in the muscles, tendons and joints and are stimulated by bodily tensions; the muscle sense.

Laterality: Of or pertaining to the side; situated at, directed towards, or coming from, the side.

Motor: Designating or pertaining to a nerve or nerve fiber which passes from the central nervous system or a ganglion to a muscle and by the impulse (motor impulse) which it transmits causes movement.

Ocular: Of, pertaining to, connected with, or used for or by the eye. Obtained, or received, by the sight; visual.

Pacing: Rate of movement.

Perceptual: Direct acquaintance with anything through the senses.

Peripheral acuity: Of, pertaining to, or constituting a periphery; hence, external; away from the central nervous system. Sharpness or acuteness of.

Potential: Existing in possibility, not in actuality; possible or in the making, as opposed to actual or realized; latent.

Spacing: Placing at intervals; arranging with spaces between.

Visual acuity: Sharpness of vision in respect to the ability to distinguish detail.

Visual awareness: Cognizant, conscious; or aware of through vision.

Visual fixation: To direct the eyes upon an object; to hold and direct steadily.

Visual steering: To direct the course of by sight. To guide, control; direct.

Visual tracking: To move in the same track as that which precedes, through vision.